32 WAYS
to become a great
SUNDAY SCHOOL TEACHER

32 WAYS
to become a great
SUNDAY
SCHOOL
TEACHER

Self-Directed Studies for Church Teachers

DELIA HALVERSON

Abingdon Press
Nashville

32 WAYS TO BECOME A GREAT SUNDAY SCHOOL TEACHER

Copyright © 1997 by Abingdon Press

This book is printed on acid-free, recycled, elemental-chlorine–free paper.

ISBN: 0-687-01787-4

259

Scripture quotations are from the New Revised Standard Version Bible, copyright © 1989, by the Division of Christian Education of the National Council of the Churches of Christ in the USA. Used by permission.

97 98 99 00 01 02 03 04 05 06 — 10 9 8 7 6 5 4 3 2 1

MANUFACTURED IN THE UNITED STATES OF AMERICA

To
those teachers who
are called
from the unknowing
to bewilderment!
To
those who live rushed
and harried lives!
YOU
are the ones who most often
become the best.

I thank God for your answer
to God's call
to
teach.

Contents

Introduction 9

The Loom: The Foundation
1. Ages and Stages 15
2. How Our Faith Develops 29
3. How to Read and Study a Bible Passage 35
4. Multiple Intelligence Learning...42
5. Why Christian Education? 47

The Warp: Personal Enrichment
6. Enriching My Prayer Life 50
7. Our Faith Story in the Bible..56
8. Simplify, Simplify!..61
9. The Bible and Teaching Faith 66
10. The Gospels..68
11. The Psalms 72
12. The Sacraments 75
13. Symbols of Christianity 79
14. Worship 84

The Weft: Practical Application
15. Death, Illness, and Other Crises...88
16. Incorporating Stewardship and Mission 94
17. Learning Centers 102
18. Lesson Planning 106
19. Positive Classroom Atmosphere 108
20. Prayer in the Classroom 114
21. Selecting Curriculum for Adults 120
22. Taking the Maze Out of Your Room.......................................123
23. Using Questions in Teaching 128
24. Teachable Moments..132
25. Teaching the Bible Creatively 136

Finishing the Fabric: Projects for Each Stage of Study
26. Observe in the Classroom 141
27. Evaluate Your Class Session 143
28. Act as Lead Teacher 145
29. Plan and Carry Out a Class Project..147
30. Compile Personal Teaching Files...150
31. Make a Permanent Teaching Aid 152
32. Prepare and Teach Observation Sessions...............................154

Appendixes
Progress Chart 157
Certificate of Accomplishment 158

Notes..159

Introduction

"When I have a whole day off, I want to spend it with my family."

"Our church is so small that we can't afford to hire someone for training."

"I have time for teacher training, but only in small increments."

"They just asked me to teach, handed me the curriculum, and said GOOD LUCK!"

"Isn't there some way I can study on my own?"

"HELP, PLEASE, SOMEBODY!"

These are some of the comments I hear as I travel around the country conducting workshops. If you are in a similar predicament, or if you just cannot make it to a training session, then this book was written for you.

For several years I have conducted self-directed studies at retreats for pastors and other leaders in Christian education. The idea for this book was sparked from those experiences, and the flame was fanned by questions and comments such as those above.

Teaching is a little like weaving a piece of fabric. A weaver must have certain equipment and materials in order to create the desired design and color. Foundational to the weaving is some sort of *loom*. It might be as complicated as a large floor loom with many places to thread the yarn, or as simple as using two branches from a tree as the foundation and simply wrapping the

yarn around them. No matter what sort of loom is used, the loom anchors the yarns with which the weaver works. The same is true with our teaching. There are certain basic foundational truths that anchor our teaching. These might be referred to as the loom.

The next material necessary for a weaver is the *vertical or warp threads* that reach from the bottom of the loom to the top. This is called the warp of the fabric, and the threads must be strong because they will have to stand up under constant use. The same is true with our teaching. Our "vertical" connection with God must be strong and durable, and the only way that we can accomplish that is by constantly deepening our faith through enrichment experiences.

Once these vertical or warp threads are strung, the weaver must use other yarns or threads to bind them together into a fabric. This is done with the *horizontal or weft threads*. These threads are wound on a shuttle or bobbin and moved in and out between the warp threads, leaving a little behind with each row. In teaching, these threads may be compared to the methods of practical application that you use in the classroom. These fibers reach out (horizontally) to your students and capture the learnings.

No piece of material can be used without the work of *finishing the fabric*. To do this, the fabric must be removed from the loom and the edges tied off; then it can be put to use. The practical application of teaching skills can be parallels this part of a weaver's works.

And so, as you learn to teach you are in many ways learning to be a weaver of the faith. In this book are the materials you will need to become a weaver of faith. God has given you a dream or a design, the basic talent to weave, and the materials with which to work. Now you can take all of these and learn how to put them together while on the job, as an apprentice.

The following sections will give you information for designing your own unique how-to course for becoming a great Sunday school teacher. In the remainder of the book you will find a variety of short studies, which have been divided into four different levels. You begin as a Student Teacher-Weaver. When that is completed (including a learning project), you move into the Apprentice Teacher-Weaver position, and then on to becoming a Worker Teacher-Weaver. As you complete the course of studies, you will be a Master Teacher-Weaver. These levels are explained on page 14.

Each of the 32 learning opportunities focuses on a specific topic that will help you become a better teacher. These are divided into weaving terms according to their goals. Each page is identified with a symbol of each of those four terms for easy reference. During each level you will work in each of the four areas. Some of them you will choose according to your own needs. Some are important to all teachers.

I hope you enjoy this learning experience as much as I have enjoyed developing and writing it.

Delia Halverson

As You Begin

Go therefore and make disciples of all nations, baptizing them in the name of the Father and of the Son and of the Holy Spirit, and teaching them to obey everything that I have commanded you. And remember, I am with you always, to the end of the age. (Matt. 28:19-20)

"Rabbi, teacher!" Jesus was called teacher no fewer than thirty-seven times in the Gospels, and we find in 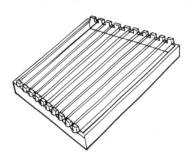 the book of Matthew alone that he was called rabbi or rabboni nine times. In Jesus' first public appearance as a leader he read the scriptures in the synagogue and then taught or interpreted them to the congregation. The last chapter of Matthew carries his commission to his disciples, affirming teachers.

Although teaching has been a part of the Christian church from the beginning, a systematic approach to Christian education for all ages is relatively new. Teaching the Christian faith may be compared to weaving. God places the design and ability in the weaver's hands, and with a loom or frame as the foundation, we teachers-weavers use various colors and fibers in the warp and weft to bring from students a fabric of faith that glorifies our Creator.

The *loom* is the frame or foundation for the weaving. It requires something steady and firm at each end. We also need a foundation for our teaching. The primary  foundation is God, for God gives us the strength and ability to carry out the mission. God also gives us the direction or the goals, which act as the remainder of the foundation for our weaving. Without God and without our direction or goals, our fabric becomes nothing but loose fibers, waving in the wind.

The *warp* threads of a fabric give it strength. Our personal enrichment through personal Bible study and prayer might be compared to the warp in the hands of the weaver. These are the threads that are secured to the loom and hold the piece steady during the weaving. Without the firm connection of the warp at the top and bottom of the loom, the woven piece easily becomes irregular and weak. As we teach, we must keep our own connection with God and recognize our goals and purpose, in order to help our students develop a strong and vibrant fabric of faith.

Often, in the finished piece, the warp is not obvious. Consequently, we sometimes ignore its value. The 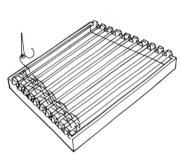 same is true in our teaching. We get so hung up in the obvious, in the physical preparation, in the weft of methods and mechanics that we forget about stringing a firm foundation with our own spiritual lives. But weaving becomes much easier when the warp is strung tightly.

Throughout the weaving process, the weaver tightens the warp to ensure a true fabric. Likewise, God can work through us in our teaching when we continually tighten those fibers of warp that keep us connected to our source.

Finally comes the *weft,* which completes the design. As the weaver slides the shuttle back and forth among the fibers of warp, a bit of the weft is left at the appropriate places, creating the design. We might consider our methods, or the different ways that we help our students learn, as the weft. The more variety we put into 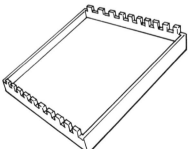 our teaching, the more the students are able to apply God's design to their lives. But each color or texture of the weft threads must be a part of the design. And each method that we use in teaching must fit into the projected learning of the student. If we throw something into the lesson just to fill up space, then it does not contribute to the plan.

Each of the learning plans in this book will be helpful to you, even if you have completed something similar, for each day finds us at a different place in our lives, ready to absorb something that seemed unimportant before. However, the following questionnaire will help you determine what you may want to concentrate on first. After finishing the questionnaire, read the next section before beginning any of the studies.

where Am I?

Read through the following statements, marking the ones that apply to you and your situation. The number after each statement corresponds to specific studies. As you plan for the alternative choices in your course, refer to those that you have marked.

My life gets too complicated. (8)

I read the Bible, but I don't seem to understand much of it. (3)

I feel that my prayer life needs help. (6)

My students don't seem to be interested in what I'm teaching. (4)

I need to make God more central in my life. (8)

I wonder why some stories are told differently by various Gospel writers. (10)

When there's a death, illness, or other crisis in my class I panic. (15)

I wish I knew more about the Psalms. (11)

My classroom needs some excitement. (22)

I appreciate Baptism and Communion, but I don't understand them. (12)

Discipline gets away from me sometimes. (19)

I wonder how my teaching will make a difference. (7)

Worship is important to me, but I wonder why we do certain things. (14)

I don't know how to include stewardship and mission in my class. (16)

I need handles on ways to make my classroom a happier place. (19)

I wonder what the Bible says about teaching. (9)

People talk about learning centers, but I'm afraid to try them. (17)

I need help in organizing my lessons. (18)

I'd like to know the important people in the Bible better. (7)

Praying in the classroom scares me. (20)

I have a hard time devising the right questions. (23)

I don't know what certain Christian symbols mean. (13)

I need new ways to teach the Bible. (25)

I wonder why we teach certain things when we do. (2)

I don't understand why some of the Psalms seem negative toward God. (11)

I wonder just what effect Christian education has on persons. (5)

I'd like to make my teaching applicable to everyday life. (24)

I'm a bit puzzled about the students I've been asked to teach. (1)

The adults in my class do not want to use curriculum. (21)

Designing Your Training

You may use the questionnaire you have just completed and the table of contents to design your own training course. In designing the course, decide on your weakest areas and concentrate your alternative subject choices in those areas.

As you go through this book you will find questions and suggestions for reflection. Use a notebook or journal for recording your thoughts. You may review your earlier thoughts from time to time. Your notes can later be placed in a personal file that will aid in your teaching.

Sharing Conversation

In order to get more out of your training, periodically meet with other teachers who are also going through this book. Discussions about the readings will help to bring out additional thoughts and creativity. Such times together will also give you support as you grow in your faith and in your teaching skills. If no other teacher is studying the course, then find another teacher or someone who has taught in the past and ask that person to be a sounding board to discuss ideas.

Time Constraints

I can't tell you exactly how long it will take for you to complete this book, because each teacher's needs are different, and we all have different time constraints. That is the advantage of a self-directed study. I would recommend that you set aside a couple of hours a week to work on this. Some of the material may be done in short bits of time, even as you wait for an appointment or in between other tasks. I do suggest, however, that when you work with the warping threads (personal enrichment), you set aside a block of time to be alone.

Additional Reading

Throughout the book you will find listings for additional reading. Read or at least become familiar with as many of these books as you can. For your future reference, compile a list or file of resources as you read. Include the name of the book, author, publisher, copyright date, and a general synopsis of the content. This will help you in future reference. Most of the books are available at bookstores, or your pastor may have some of them. Or check with your local church library or another agency of your church. If several teachers are using this book, it would benefit your church to purchase the additional reading books for a teacher resource library.

How the Book Is Divided

As a weaver needs various tools to weave a fabric, we teachers need various areas of learning and experience as we develop our ministry. The 32 studies are in four areas:

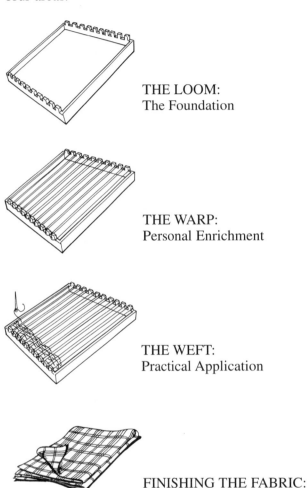

THE LOOM:
The Foundation

THE WARP:
Personal Enrichment

THE WEFT:
Practical Application

FINISHING THE FABRIC:
Projects for Each Stage of Study

The training stages are also divided into four levels. Beginning teachers may find that they need to spend more time on each level. In keeping with the concept of weaving, each level of the teacher-weaver includes studies from the loom, the warp, and weft, and with a project.

Student Teacher-Weaver
Apprentice Teacher-Weaver
Worker Teacher-Weaver
Master Teacher-Weaver

Study Plan

Note: Courses with an asterisk (*) should be studied. Select optional ones from table of Contents.

Student Teacher-Weaver

You may begin with this training level if you have never taught a class or even if you are an experienced veteran. If you are a new teacher, this level will provide you with a framework or foundation of understanding. For an experienced teacher, the Student Teacher-Weaver level will generate new insights in your teaching ministry.

Two or three studies from the Loom (Foundational), pages 15-49.
- [ ]* Why Christian Education?
- [ ]* Ages and Stages (all ages).

One choice from the Warp (Enrichment), pages 50-87.
- [ ] _____

Two choices from the Weft (Application), pages 88-140.
- [ ] _____
- [ ] _____

One or two choices from the following Finishings (Projects), pages 141-55.
- [ ] Observe in Classroom (necessary for new teachers).
- [ ] Evaluate Your Own Class Session.

Apprentice Teacher-Weaver

One or two studies from the Loom (Foundational), pages 15-49.
- [ ]* How Faith Grows.
- [ ] How to Read and Study Bible Passages (optional).
- [ ] _____

One choice from the Warp (Enrichment), pages 50-87.
- [ ] _____

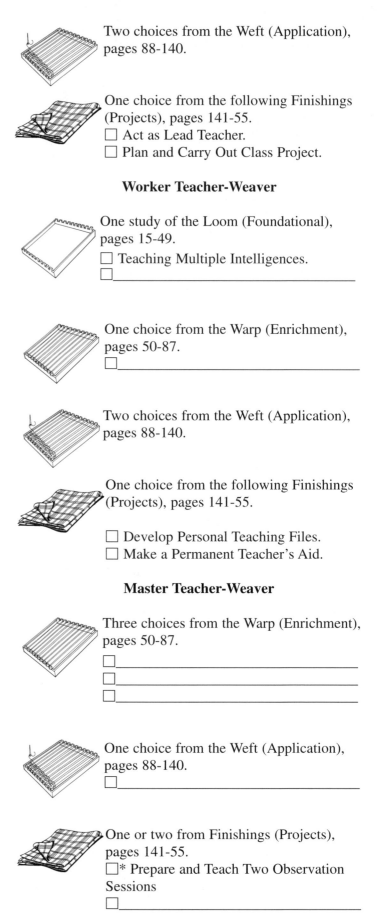

Two choices from the Weft (Application), pages 88-140.

One choice from the following Finishings (Projects), pages 141-55.
- [ ] Act as Lead Teacher.
- [ ] Plan and Carry Out Class Project.

Worker Teacher-Weaver

One study of the Loom (Foundational), pages 15-49.
- [ ] Teaching Multiple Intelligences.
- [ ] _____

One choice from the Warp (Enrichment), pages 50-87.
- [ ] _____

Two choices from the Weft (Application), pages 88-140.

One choice from the following Finishings (Projects), pages 141-55.

- [ ] Develop Personal Teaching Files.
- [ ] Make a Permanent Teacher's Aid.

Master Teacher-Weaver

Three choices from the Warp (Enrichment), pages 50-87.
- [ ] _____
- [ ] _____
- [ ] _____

One choice from the Weft (Application), pages 88-140.
- [ ] _____

One or two from Finishings (Projects), pages 141-55.
- [ ]* Prepare and Teach Two Observation Sessions
- [ ] _____

THE LOOM: THE FOUNDATION

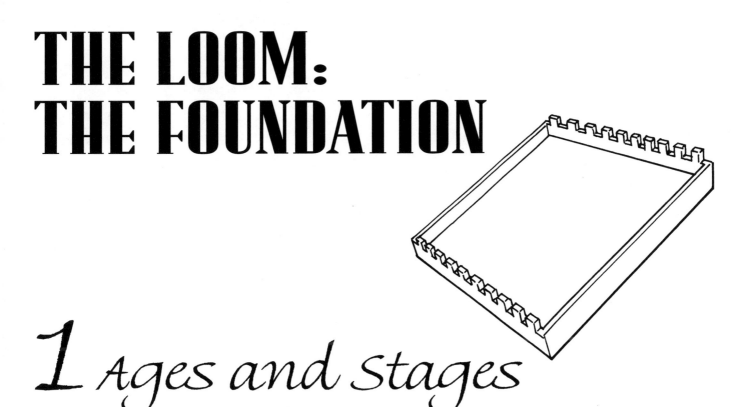

1 Ages and Stages

Purpose: To grasp a better understanding of the students in order to plan for reaching them with the message of Christ.

Jesus taught us that we must listen to and get to know our students. He exhibited this when he adapted his teachings to the Pharisees and scribes, using references to the scriptures and to other people, through common, everyday objects and events.

☐ Read Mark 7:1-13 and Mark 12:13-17.

☐ When did Jesus use other common-life objects or events?

_____

_____

_____

☐ Jesus also listened to his students and adapted his teachings to their needs. Read Matthew 15:21-28.

Whether we teach children, youth, or adults, we cannot do an effective job if we do not learn to understand our students. This section covers all ages, giving not only characteristics but also faith concepts (pages 26-27) appropriate for the younger ages. When considering faith concepts for youth and adults, see "How Our

Faith Develops" (Study #2, page 29).

Read through all age levels on the chart that follows. This will not only help you know your students, but also give you an idea of where they have been in their faith development and where they are headed. It will also help you to understand their parents, or their children or grandchildren.

After reading through the information, think about these questions:

☐ Which characteristics best fit the majority of your students?

_____

_____

_____

☐ What students in your class have special needs that differ from those of most of the others in your class (such as individual attention, help with a specific skill, encouragement to speak out, etc.)? List the names of these students and their needs.

15

Name	Needs
_____	_____
_____	_____
_____	_____ .
_____	_____

☐ What are some ways that you can let your students know that you think each of them is special (such as complimenting someone on an article of clothing, asking about the health of a family member, etc.)?

_____

_____

_____

Additional Resources

☐ Review or read some of these additional resources.

Barna, George. *Generation NeXt.* Barna Res. Group.

Halverson, Delia. *Leading Adult Learners.* Nashville: Abingdon Press, 1995.

Hartman, Warren J. *Five Audiences.* Nashville: Abingdon Press, 1987.

Miller, Craig. *Baby Boomer Spirituality.* Nashville: Discipleship Resources.

———. *Postmoderns.* Nashville: Discipleship Resources.

Miller, Karen. *Ages and Stages.* West Palm Beach, Fla.: Telshare, 1985.

Children Differ

The infant **may be like this:**

- wiggles, squirms, squeals, and kicks—grasps for items.
- smiles for strangers as well as family.
- crawls or rolls from one place to another.
- responds in individual ways.

The infant needs:

- to be loved and cared for and kept dry and changed.
- an environment that is safe and clean (and nontoxic).
- adults who recognize the child's behavior and offer encouragement.
- room for crawling and objects to hold and grasp.
- items to watch and follow with eyes.

Parents of infants need:

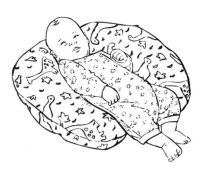

- to know the environment is clean and safe and the child is cared for and loved.
- to be called by name and recognized.
- to know that you have concern when the child is ill.
- to be assured that the child's interest is yours.

The toddler and two-year-old **may be like this:**

- are beginning to know the power of saying "no."
- are fearless in trying new things.
- climb or step on to get where they want to be.
- begin to match words with objects.
- toddler has special language of own; two-year-old begins to drop the special language.
- are unable to comprehend pronouns (Jimmy kick the ball instead of "I").
- may hit or attack peers when cannot communicate with words.
- play well beside, instead of with, others; everything is "me" centered.
- have very short attention span.

Two-year-old particularly:

- has beginning capabilities of some creative activities.
- often prefers adult relationships to peer.
- can recall events of yesterday, missing toys, etc.
- uses color names but unable to identify yet.
- uses numbers and words to accompany serial pointing, serving as foundation for later discriminative counting.
- talks while acts and acts while talks.
- can't fold paper well yet, but enjoys using paper.
- begins process thinking (pushes chair to climb up to get something).
- growing sense of possession displayed by hiding toys to have later.
- shows off to adults and peers to make them laugh.
- shows affection spontaneously.
- mimics adult expressions of emotion.
- dawdles often.
- considers self "older" than younger child.

The toddler and two-year-old need:

- adults who keep constant check on actions and offer comfort.
- routine to give them stability.
- adults who do first, and then explain as they do it again.
- room to move about and have individual play.
- motion activities to satisfy muscular development.
- to hear others tell stories about them and familiar belongings.
- listeners and encouragement in developing communication skills.
- help with words to show emotions. "You are *angry* because . . ."
- opportunity to express possessiveness.

17

- pictures at eye level, two or three feet above floor, and low shelves within reach.
- songs and games with repetition and imitation.
- multiple toys (where possible) for parallel play; nontoxic materials.
- nearby bathroom facilities for two-year-olds.
- opportunity to see creative accomplishment for two-year-olds.

Parents of toddlers and two-year-olds need:
- to know that the environment is clean and safe, and that child is cared for and loved.
- to be called by name and recognized.
- to know that you have concern when the child is ill.
- to become involved with child's class.
- to be assured child's interest is yours and you love the child even when there are problems.

The three-year-old may be like this:
- enjoys motor activity, but less than twos.
- enjoys finger manipulations with play materials.
- likes to use crayons but unable to stay in lines well.
- drawing is more directed with some controlled marks (not controlled well enough to draw a person).
- delights in scissors; begins cutting "fringes" around edges of paper and then cutting across paper; cutting out pictures comes with more practice.
- has longer attention span.
- builds tower of nine to ten blocks.
- folds paper lengthwise and crosswise, but not diagonally.
- can pedal, jump upward, balance on one foot for short time.
- starts and stops easily and makes sharp turns.
- begins to recognize forms.
- is sometimes rather tidy and orderly.
- sentences become longer and has many questions.
- words are now instruments for relating ideas, concepts, relationships, etc.
- enjoys creating chants.
- tries to use muscles to solve problem instead of thinking ability (will try to force puzzle piece instead of turning it around).
- has sense of incompleteness, fragments (turns page of a book for more of a story, etc.).
- begins to classify, compare things.
- is learning to listen but still enjoys being listened to.
- is beginning bargaining ability—sacrificing something now for later.
- has strong desire to please.
- talks to self and imaginary persons.
- enjoys other children, but still needs solitary and parallel play.
- begins to understand waiting turns and sharing.
- may ask questions to which already knows answer.

The three-year-old needs:
- beginning finger plays.
- simple rhythm instrument opportunities (may be homemade).
- to watch forms being drawn to imitate.
- opportunities to "do it myself."
- materials for development of smaller muscles, along with some big muscles.
- adults who are sensitive to inner feelings, who may cover embarrassment.
- appreciation for contributions to community living.
- understanding, tolerance, and acceptance of different development levels.
- to be told about the unknown and what causes things.
- modeling of Christian values.

Parents of three-year-olds need:
- to be called by name and recognized.
- to know that you have concern when the child is ill.
- to know that the environment is clean and safe.
- to know that the child is cared for and loved.

- to become involved with their child's class.
- to be assured the child's interest is yours and that you love the child even when there are problems.
- encouragement when their child develops differently from others.

The four-year-old may be like this:
- runs, stops, turns with ease.
- may be able to skip and stand on one leg for a period of time.
- throws and catches ball or bean bag; swings without help.
- can recognize and reproduce body movements.
- strings large and small beads (not very small) and follows simple patterns.
- copies circle, triangle, square; matches colors and shapes.
- claps hands in imitation of simple rhythm.
- can use brushes at easel properly.
- cuts on straight line and some simple outlines; simple paper folding.
- recognizes simple alike and different objects.
- identifies missing parts if not too complex.
- memory is developing for two- to four-color or object sequence.
- recognizes own name; knows first and last name.
- recognizes and matches various environmental sounds.
- retells very short stories accurately; recalls jingles, rhymes, etc.
- using language, communicates needs and begins to solve problems.
- has little comprehension of past and future.
- thinks literally; is baffled by storyteller analogies.
- worships God, although cannot verbally explain (in awe of creation).
- likes to go from one thing to another rather than repeat.
- constantly questions; much chattering (sometimes for attention).
- is more bossy and mature than threes, but enjoys groups of two to three children.
- shares possessions and suggests turns, but does not play orderly.

The four-year-old needs:
- simple rhythm instrument opportunities (may be homemade).
- opportunities to "do it myself."
- adults sensitive to inner feelings, who may cover embarrassment.
- appreciation for contributions to community living.
- understanding, tolerance, and acceptance of different development levels.
- to be told about the unknown and what causes things.
- modeling of Christian values.
- opportunities to extend social development.
- persons who talk literally.
- frequent opportunities to move about without undue pressure.
- opportunities for quiet reflection.

Parents of four-year-olds need:
- to be called by name and recognized.
- to know that you have concern when the child is ill.
- to know that the environment is clean and safe.
- to know that the child is cared for and loved.
- to become involved with child's class.
- to be assured child's interest is yours and you love the child even when there are problems.
- encouragement to follow up on class activities at home.

The five-year-old may be like this:
- is active most of time, but fatigues quickly.
- has better-developed large muscles; is developing better small muscles.
- exhibits slower physical growth than in previous years.
- responds to routine and organization with some interest in organized games.
- plans and plays together in small groups.
- has incomplete eye development (is often farsighted).

- left- or right-handedness is usually established.
- handles personal needs (eating, toilet, some dressing, etc.).
- is jealous of other children; competes for adult attention.
- has strong link to parents, particularly mother; may return to younger behavior.
- begins to look for reason for authority.
- exhibits developing sense of humor.
- is becoming cooperative and helpful, but will argue and become angry.
- enjoys small responsibilities and thrives on praise and affection.
- copies authority figures in play (parents, teacher, etc.)
- expects rules and limits to be literal; sometimes confuses fact and fantasy.
- has better understanding of sequence of events but little concept of time.
- is developing respect for rights of others.
- has little understanding of cause and effect.
- has "special" friend, or feels left out because has no "special" friend.

The five-year-old needs:
- simple answers to the many questions asked.
- firsthand experiences to gain new information.
- simple opportunities to make generalizations and see relationships.
- guidance in new skill of making thoughtful decisions.
- adults sensitive to inner feelings, and who may cover embarrassment.
- praise for accomplishments and contributions to group living.
- modeling of Christian values.
- persons who talk literally instead of abstractly.
- opportunities for quiet reflection.
- to be recognized by teacher in community (at grocery store, etc.).
- to feel needed, with assigned "helper/steward" or leader positions.
- activities that involve the senses.
- people who will listen with ears and eyes.
- changes in pace—active followed by quiet.

Parents of five-year-olds need:
- to be called by name and recognized.
- to know that you have concern when the child is ill.
- to know that the child is cared for and loved.
- encouragement when their child develops differently from others.
- to become involved with child's class.
- to be assured child's interest is yours and you love the child even when there are problems.
- encouragement to follow up on class activities at home.

The younger elementary boy or girl **may be like this:**
- is restless, active, and energetic but still tires easily.
- experiences slow physical development as body growth stabilizes.
- takes less interest in own body as physical being; not yet conscious of sexual being.
- likes to learn by doing.
- discouraged if unable to complete a project because of lack of time or skill.
- math skills improving, but still needs concrete terms.
- by grade three is beginning map reading skills and understands some history.
- by second grade is beginning cursive writing.
- has attention span of ten to fifteen minutes.
- is beginning to manipulate symbols mentally, without use of hands or objects.
- is beginning to read, but reading at different levels.
- is beginning to reason from own experience.
- is rule-bound (everything is right or wrong; "fair" means "equal").
- reasoning skill is increasing.
- reflects parental attitudes.
- has vivid imagination and enjoys dramatization.
- likes stories, read to or to read.

- "me-ism" develops toward others (God loves me—I love others).
- interests of boys and girls often differ.
- enjoys "best friend" but may shift friends; peer cliques and clubs shift easily.

The younger elementary boy or girl needs:
- "real" tools and equipment rather than toys.
- opportunities to be with people of all ages and playmates of both sexes.
- opportunities to explore meaning of Bible stories to own life.
- opportunities to use art forms and words to convey ideas and feelings.
- simple interpretation of symbols although the younger elementary child may not grasp them.
- pride of owning "own" Bible and help in learning to use it.
- opportunity to do own planning and solve own problems.
- conversation, songs, and stories to help learn some Bible verses.
- free dramatic play and spontaneous dramatization.
- adults who point out child's positive physical and personality characteristics.
- sympathy when emotionally hurt but encouragement to forget quickly.
- projects broken down into small tasks, and understanding when the child fails at things beyond ability.
- experiences with life cycles and relating these to God as Creator.
- encouragement to ask "how" and "why," although the child generally accepts almost everything told about God.
- opportunities for quiet reflection.

Parents of younger elementary children need:
- to be called by name and recognized.
- to know that you have concern when the child is ill.
- to prepare for child's loyalty to switch from parents to peers.
- to become involved with child's class.
- to be assured child's interest is yours and you love the child even when there are problems.
- encouragement to follow up on class activities at home.

The older elementary boy or girl **may be like this:**
- is increasingly interested in peer group, in forming "clubs" and "gangs"; looking to peers for authority more than adults; tending to accept without question the values of the group;
- growing interest, especially among girls, in the opposite sex; many, especially boys, may continue to prefer activities with own sex.
- is increasingly independent, wanting to make own decisions.
- is interested in perfecting skills.
- experiences a spurt in growth, especially in girls; may feel awkward, gawky, embarrassed; late growers may be anxious, be called "Shrimp," "Tiny," etc.
- thinks about what he or she will do when grown up.
- is increasingly able to think abstractly, to reason, to grasp the relation of cause and effect; is skeptical, questioning about matters of faith accepted earlier.
- feels intensely about fair play and justice.
- is informed and concerned about people and conditions around the world.
- has increased attention span (fifteen to twenty minutes).

The older elementary boy or girl needs:
- many wholesome, meaningful activities in a group in which the child has a sense of belonging; encouragement to do things with individuals and groups whose values are desirable, to develop an independent set of values.
- opportunity to make own decisions where appropriate, to share in determining plans and procedures of own church group.
- adults who expect the best the child is able to produce, who provide opportunity to master skills in which the child shows interest.
- adults who help the child understand and accept individual growth "timetables."
- opportunity to explore many possible occupations, to develop a sense of Christian vocation (direction of life) used later in deciding about occupation.
- encouragement to express honest skepticism; adults who affirm their own faith, help children do their own thinking, and do not expect them to believe as they themselves believe.

- adults who are fair and just in their relations with others, who help boys and girls see the implications of their faith for their personal and social relations.
- opportunity to engage directly and indirectly in the worldwide ministry of their church.
- opportunity to worship, learn, and play with persons of all ages.

Parents of older elementary children need:
- to be called by name and recognized.
- to know that you have concern when the child is ill.
- understanding that children are transferring allegiance from adults to peers.
- understanding that inquiring into our faith is a natural development process.
- to become involved with child's class.
- to be assured child's interest is yours and you love the child even when there are problems.
- encouragement to follow up on class activities at home.

The middle schooler **may be like this:**
- experiences varying developmental changes; some develop more rapidly than others; those on the leading edge sometimes feel ahead, and those who change less rapidly feel inadequate.
- usually experiences a sudden growth spurt in height; when this happens faster in girls than in boys it causes great differences in the sexes.
- feels awkwardness as learns to handle bigger hands, feet, shoulders, hips.
- is unaware of the increase in physical strength.
- has great need to look "like" peers; attractiveness is of great concern.
- experiments with various roles, personalities, values, etc.
- is trying to break away from parental ties and develop peer ties.
- feels anxiety over personal identity.
- fluctuates between lack of self-esteem and good self-esteem.
- is moving from concrete thought into more general, abstract, and symbolic thought; but some still think concretely.
- reading levels vary greatly.
- most have short attention span; many learn better through electronic media.
- is feeling isolated with limited ability to communicate.
- vacillates between dependence and independence.
- is moving from using rules only for own purposes and concrete punishment, to recognizing that our roles and action affect everyone.
- is questioning the literal faith of childhood and accepting conventional faith.
- religious knowledge is minimal and poorly organized.

The middle schooler needs:
- many and varied learning opportunities that are active and gamelike.
- opportunity to choose activities, whether to read, play games, etc.
- studies and programs that deal with *his* or *her* everyday problems.
- opportunity to engage directly and indirectly in the worldwide ministry of the church.
- adults who don't play favorites and who talk to everyone in group.
- adults who will not embarrass him or her in front of others.
- adults who set an example of not making fun of other people.
- adults who ask "What do you think?" and really listen and accept answer.
- encouragement in new thought process.
- affirmation when the student has accomplished something.
- recognition when encountered in the community.
- persons who will listen without "offering advice" unless asked, and then it's better to help the middle schooler come up with his own answers.
- adults who share their own beliefs, but do not force them upon the middle schooler.
- opportunities to develop a real sense of belonging to the group.

Parents of middle schoolers need:
- to know just what's happening in class plans and activities and when.
- to know that their child is under constant supervision.
- to have regular opportunities for discussion with leaders.
- help in understanding their middle schooler.
- opportunity to be a part of the program.

The high schooler **may be like this:**
- questions the desire to be an individual or part of the crowd.
- is individually different in age and pace of change.
- growth levels off for most and growing acceptance of own body.
- is better able to manage strength and coordination.
- may resist commitments, wanting to be open to what future may bring.
- the ethnic youth sometimes becomes personally concerned with cultural awareness.
- select peer groups become more important, consume majority of waking hours.
- some catch up physically with others; sexual fantasies often evident with pressure for experimentation; searching for sexual identification.
- establishing role models that may or may not remain models in future.
- leadership roles become more evident and sometimes create conflicts.
- has both same-sex and opposite-sex friendships, many one-on-one.
- some become "closer friends" to parents and some develop more conflict; this relationship often mellows in later years.
- adult-to-adult relationships begin to develop with adults outside family, particularly in later years.
- some are reviewing established rules.
- some are inquiring into their faith, while others continue to accept specifics simply because they were "instructed" in them in the past.
- some find excitement in learning while others are bored.
- experience wide range of differences between ninth and twelfth grades.
- school activities and sports are often important.
- begin wage-paying jobs, which give them self-esteem but pressure them for time.
- most now drive and many have cars, giving them more independence.
- some accept stereotypes, but many reject them.
- most can concentrate and enjoy longer times of idea exchanges.
- most are willing to try new ideas.
- some continue to seem flighty and unpredictable, but many take on responsibility and can manage difficult tasks.

The high schooler needs:
- many and varied active learning opportunities.
- opportunity to help shape their own activities and their own group direction.
- programs that are life-centered, with biblical background.
- opportunity to engage directly or indirectly in worldwide ministry of church.
- adults who accept their ideas as valid and don't embarrass them.
- adults who affirm their own faith, encouraging them to think for themselves.
- adults who will "search" with them for answers.
- persons who will listen and accept their ideas as valid.
- adults who will help them develop their global understanding.
- opportunities to develop a sense of importance in the church.
- affirmation and recognition for accomplishment.
- opportunities to use their forming leadership abilities.

Parents of high schoolers need:
- to know just what's happening in class plans and activities and when.
- to have regular opportunities for discussion with leaders.
- help in knowing how to prepare their high schooler for independent life.
- opportunities to be a part of the program.

Adult Generations

Generation X'ers **may be like this:**
- were born during the sixties, seventies, and early eighties.
- are also called the 13th Generation (13th generation of American citizens), Baby Busters (numbers of births down), and the Lost or Gap Generation.
- were born of parents who looked out for #1 and had no firm religious convictions.
- products of contraceptives, two-income families, changing sex roles, limited resources, violent role models,

mobile lifestyles, declining job markets.
- many from homes of plenty, but many also from homes below poverty level.
- a generation with average income of $10,000, many without jobs.
- expected to have greatest impact on money and marketplace.

Characteristics of Generation X'ers are:
- independent; view themselves as realists and survivors, risk takers.
- skeptical of people; let down by national role figures they admired.
- flexible; anxious to cut to the action without wasting time talking.
- work at jobs to enjoy leisure and expect to have several careers in life.
- slow to commit to marriage and raising children but hope for stable family life.
- good at finding alternative ways around impossible situations.

Generation X'ers want from a church:
- redefinition of Christian values; life can be abundant without abundance.
- willingness to listen and offer understanding, but encouragement to seek their *own* answers and make their *own* decisions.
- pragmatic Christianity, including *all* of life.
- involvement of laity in experiential study, worship leadership, and decisions with action.
- biblical emphasis on survival during hardships.
- experiential learning with practical applications to any spiritual decisions.
- opportunity for hands-on mission to persons *before* learning about Christ.
- discussions *after* doing or after active learning experiences.
- action rather than polite conversation about ideologies.
- multiple worship styles involving senses, time frames, small support groups, styles and locations for study, service to others, leadership opportunities.
- images of God's diversity.

Baby Boomers **may be like this:**
- were born 1946–1964.
- are one in three Americans.
- have 3-D lifestyle:
  Delayed marriage
  Deferred childbearing
  Divorcing couples.
- often dictate change because of their sheer numbers.
- not all are swinging and rich: many average $15,000 or less in income.
- are generally unchurched and biblically illiterate.
- were baptized as infants.
- few joined a church.
- are questioning, as they enter midlife.

Characteristics of Baby Boomers are:
- two-income families.
- moms pulled between moving up in career and family devotion.
- dads more involved with children.
- materialistic models—adult peer pressure.
- no dedication to one denomination or church.
- tight schedules.

Baby Boomers want in a church:
- innovative worship.
- involvement *before* joining.
- family involvement.
- consideration of pressed and erratic time schedules (suppers, child care, meeting times clustered, etc.).
- short-term assignments and studies.
- options provided.
- opportunity to develop common bonds, support systems.
- because of limited time, they want their time to be fulfilled, not just filled.
- opportunity to help in an area of their interest.

- evidence that their commitment makes a difference.
- service that is people-oriented, rather than task-oriented.
- awareness of and help for the oppressed; mission support (money and hands-on).
- support for global peace.
- more than informational Bible study, study that affects their lives.

Silent Generation **adults may be like this:**
- were born 1925–1942.
- raised during the Depression, World War II.
- were born too soon or too late.
- had early marriage, early childbearing.
- experience dilemma over feminism.
- experience personal (not national) passages.

Characteristics of the Silent Generation are:
- arbitrators, mediators.
- adaptive but slow decisions.
- directed to others.
- assisting roles, public life.
- like to deliberate.
- gather facts, opinions.
- prefer process to outcome.

The Silent Generation wants in the church:
- advocacy opportunities.
- time to reflect before making decisions.
- help with life situations.
- discussion opportunities.
- praise for leadership.
- change with reason.
- people-oriented service.

GI Generation **adults may be like this:**
- were born 1901–1924.
- went from horse and buggy to space travel.
- experienced two world wars.
- had one-income families.
- believe strongly in civic and government institutions.

Characteristics of the GI Generation are:
- self-sufficient, aggressive.
- strong values.
- powerful work ethic.
- believe in institutions.
- strong denominational ties.
- resist change.

The GI Generation wants in the church:
- belonging in community.
- loyalty.
- ownership, personal space.
- strong Bible study.
- emphasis on values.
- consistent traditions.
- attention to detail.[1]

25

THE CHILD/THE CONCEPT

	YOUNG PRESCHOOL	OLDER PRESCHOOL	GRADES 1-3	GRADES 4-6
GOD	Associate God with beautiful things. Enjoy creating with God. Associate God with love and care that parents and other adults give. Use the term "God." (The only father the child knows is Daddy.) Encourage the growing desire to talk to God in brief, direct, and simple prayers, as if God were here beside us.	Point out God's plan of cycles. God is dependable. Day follows night; spring always comes. Stress that God planned night for rest and day for work. Give examples of God's plan for growing. Stress that God loves us and gives us good things. Because God loves us, God wants to be loved by us in return and wants us to share. Teach concept of how God cares for us through others (doctors, farmers, etc.). Stress that we can show our love for God by the things we do. Build on nursery-age concepts.	Explain that because God is good and we are God's children, God expects us to be good. We are good because we love God, not because we are afraid of punishment. Explain that God forgives us; we forgive others. Help the child to learn to right wrongs. Stress that God helps us get through problems. Say that we help carry out God's purposes by working with God's laws; if we don't get enough sleep, we will get sick; if we are kind to people, they are happy and life is happy for us.	Explain that we help God's balance in nature. Assure children that God's laws will not change. God's justice is part of God's love. Stress that God depends on responsible people. Introduce the child to God as the parent of all peoples; God is all-wise and all-good. Explain that if we fail, God is sorry but still loves us. Build confidence in God's forgiveness when we are truly sorry. Say that God helps through the wisdom of older persons and the lives of many people. Stress that God helps through the Bible. Explain that we learn more about God's world each day.
JESUS	Talk about Jesus, the man who loved children. Say that Jesus told people what God is like. Christmas: Remember when Jesus was a baby; begin with the man Jesus and remember. Easter: Stress new life and loving and appreciating Jesus. Use separate identities of Jesus and God.	Tell stories of Jesus, who helped and loved others. Stress that we learn from Jesus. Say that whenever we do things Jesus would do and act as he did, we act as his friends. Emphasize that Easter is a time for remembering Jesus. Encourage growth in love for Jesus. Retain separate identities of Jesus and God. Enjoy dressing as people did in Jesus' day.	Say that Jesus was sent to show us the love of God. Encourage a desire to be like Jesus. Encourage the beginning of an understanding of Jesus as ever living and helping today. Talk about the segments of the life of Jesus: teacher, friend, concerned with others' health. Talk about customs of Bible times. Begin discussing the Hebrew heritage. Easter: Near the upper end of this age-group, tell briefly that some people didn't like Jesus' teachings and they put him to death, but his friends felt he was still near. Tell the *story* of the Resurrection; however, the next age-group deals better with physical or spiritual aspects of resurrection. Retain separate identities of Jesus and God but move toward the Grades 4-6 concept.	Make a conscious effort to use Jesus' teachings every day. Tell about Jesus' life chronologically. Talk about the spiritual difference Jesus' life made—he made a better world. Show Jesus as a hero. Point out that Jesus showed us God. Some believe he was God, some that he was a man who let God work through him. Talk of your own belief, but let the child develop his or her belief. Help child to realize that this is not something that must be decided immediately. The important thing is that Jesus showed us God and God's ways for us to live. (Older children can grasp the idea that through Jesus God experienced human life and therefore can better help us.)
PRAYER	Pray prayers of thanksgiving and praise. Associate prayer with good things. Pray with the child as if you are talking to God. Begin the relationship with God. Use simple language: "you" and "your," not "thee," "thou," and "thine." No particular body position is necessary. Child need not always close eyes. Giving thanks for food after eating makes more sense to this age child.	Provide some opportunities for prayer. Pray spontaneous prayers. "Talk" to God. Prayer can be two to five short sentences of everyday speech. Pray with words the child understands. Religion is private; prayer is not a time to show off. Be cautious of asking child to pray before guests. Evening prayers: Talk over happy times of the day, kindnesses, how God helped—then pray. Begin requests for help: "Help me to remember to cross the street carefully . . . to take turns . . . to help others." Older kindergarteners may pray for someone else: "Help the doctor to help Johnny." Begin to distinguish between asking Daddy for toys and asking God to help us take turns. God works through people for physical needs.	Continue praise and thanksgiving. Let the child compose his or her own written prayers. Create litany prayers together. Give opportunities for sentence prayers after discussion of what we are thankful for—don't force the child to pray. Acknowledge need for forgiveness. Encourage prayers asking for help, making them more specific than before.	Encourage personal and private worship. Provide devotional material. Help child to appreciate prayers in formal worship. Study prayers in hymnal for special occasions. Continue prayer as close relationship with God. Encourage growth so that this relationship with God is in place when child is more independent.

YOUNG PRESCHOOL	OLDER PRESCHOOL	GRADES 1-3	GRADES 4-6

CHURCH

YOUNG PRESCHOOL	OLDER PRESCHOOL	GRADES 1-3	GRADES 4-6
Stress happy experiences at church —with other children, —with church workers, —with other classes. Begin association of God and Jesus with the church. Review the prayers prayed and stories heard at church. Visit sanctuary during nonservice time. Introduce the word *steward* as one who helps and cares.	Encourage growing enjoyment of child's part in church. Help child to feel that this is his or her church. Find ways to let the child help workers in the church. Speak of the child as "steward of the plants" when watering plants, etc. Begin to learn the Lord's Prayer and worship responses. Help child to be responsible for things: arranging chairs, sharing money gifts for the things we need at church. Continue association of God and Jesus with church.	Encourage involvement of the church in the community (shut-ins). Encourage giving gifts of service for the church: to missionaries, toys for the nursery, etc. Introduce stewardship of money. Provide offering envelopes and pledge cards. Share with church workers. Point out that God's house is like our home—we keep it clean. Appreciate the sanctuary and experiences there. Encourage interest in the ongoing program of the church. Visit the office, see records; see the furnace room, electric meter, cleaning equipment; view order forms for literature. (Say that we give money to help with these things.) Talk with the minister about how the minister uses his or her car, books that are needed, and the fact that he or she has a family. Point out that if the minister is to give his or her days to the church, we must pay to help provide for the minister's family.	Recognize the developing understanding of the worship service, sacraments, and creeds. Appreciate all sections of the hymnal. Begin to appreciate the church symbols; point out that symbols were used to remind people of Bible stories before everyone could read the Bible. Talk about the heritage of the church to the present day. Expand knowledge of the church as the church exists around the world. Stress that there are different churches because there are different beliefs. We all believe in God. Introduce the term "ecumenical."

BIBLE

YOUNG PRESCHOOL	OLDER PRESCHOOL	GRADES 1-3	GRADES 4-6
Use simple verses at spontaneous times. Hold the Bible and tell simple stories: children visiting Jesus; Jesus teaching about God; Jesus enjoying nature; Jesus having breakfast at the lake with friends; Jesus' babyhood; Mary and Joseph caring for Jesus. Avoid stories of violence.	Add stories of Jesus' friends. Tell Old Testament stories that exemplify positive behavior: Miriam's care of her baby brother; Samuel's new coat (his saying "thank you"); Ruth gathering grain and sharing with Naomi; preparing a rooftop room to welcome a visitor. Associate everyday stories with what we learn from the Bible. Use longer, understandable verses. Read verses, using a translation the child can understand. Begin Bible/God association.	Make Bible reading a pleasant experience. Be sure passages are simple. Provide opportunities to learn the background from which the Bible comes. Encourage using the Bible in solving our everyday problems. Relate our life to situations in Bible stories: Now we have no roofs to sit on and watch stars—we sit on the deck or in our backyard. We still can enjoy sleeping in tents as in Bible times. Jesus helped the lonely—we help new children in school. Tell about the two parts of the Bible: Old Testament (or Hebrew scripture) that Joseph read to his family and Jesus enjoyed; New Testament (or scripture of the Christian era) that tells about Jesus and his friends. Tell about the Psalms, the hymnbook of the Bible. By grade 3, begin teaching to use verses and chapters.	Provide a historical approach to the Bible. Look at the Bible's table of contents; group the books; use the maps. Help child to learn to live by the principles of the Bible. Help child to evaluate own behavior by looking at Jesus' life. Begin to use Old Testament stories showing wrong behavior. Point out that the Old Testament relates growth of Jewish understanding of God and that the New Testament adds to this knowledge. Tell stories about the early church. Show that the New Testament records how Jesus' friends told others about him. From 32 WAYS TO BECOME A GREAT SUNDAY SCHOOL TEACHER by Delia Halverson. Copyright © 1997 by Abingdon Press. Reproduced by permission.

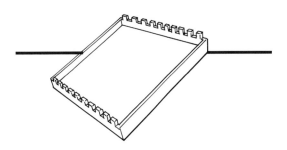

2 How Our Faith Develops

PURPOSE: To understand the faith process and recognize how the teacher influences that process.

Faith and our beliefs can be confused. Our beliefs are understandings that we hold to be true. As we experience the world, sometimes we begin to see things differently. These beliefs, then, may change from time to time throughout our lives. Faith, on the other hand, can be defined as our relationship with God. As this relationship with God deepens, our faith matures.

God becomes known to us in as many ways as there are people. Since God made each of us unique, we each experience God differently.

☐ Read Acts 9:1-19 for Paul's experience with God.

☐ Read 2 Timothy 1:3-9 for Paul's affirmation of persons being nurtured in the faith from childhood.

How did the experiences of Paul and Timothy differ?

_____

_____

_____

Some of us have Paul's kind of experience with God, and some of us slowly grow in our relationship with God, as Timothy did. Paul's letter to Timothy affirms his gradual growth in relationship with God.

☐ Recall some high points in the past when you felt closest to God.

_____

_____

_____

In order to help you better understand your own faith journey and how God becomes a part of your everyday life, prayerfully complete the following suggestions.

Experiential Faith

☐ With pictures, symbols, or words, record a time when you felt physically or emotionally warm as a child.

Although you did not recognize it at the time, these experiences were beginning foundations for your faith formation, particularly what might be called our **experiential faith.**

29

☐ List some ways that you can create opportunities for your students to deepen their experiential faith:

_____

_____

_____

_____

_____

Affiliated Faith

☐ Remember persons who helped you to understand God better throughout your life. Some of them may have told you Bible stories, or they may have encouraged you to talk about your beliefs. Write something about those persons below.

_____

_____

_____

_____

_____

John H. Westerhoff III, in his book *Will Our Children Have Faith?* suggests that we may move through four styles of faith. The first, experiential faith, includes times we experience God, sometimes through others or through experiences that other people prepare for us. From the first time that an infant is brought to the church, and held and rocked in the nursery, to the caring touch that means so much to a dying person, we experience God's love through other people. The Sunday school curriculum also helps our faith to grow when it includes experiential activities that relate to the theme. Through these experiences we grow in our understanding and relationship with God.

Another part of our experiential faith is awe and worship of God. When you build opportunities for worship into your classroom experience and grasp moments of wonder, you enable students' faith to deepen.

God made us to be in relationship with God and with other persons. The persons you just listed are a part of your own **affiliated faith.** Through our relationships with other Christians, and by claiming them as our family of God, we are active in our affiliated style of faith. As a teacher, one of your primary tasks is to help the students to build relationships.

☐ List some ways that you can deepen the affiliated faith of your students:

_____

_____

_____

_____

Searching or Inquiring Faith

☐ Use pictures, symbols, or words to recall a belief you had as a child that you no longer hold to be true (example: that God zaps us or sits on a cloud).

Most people move into a **searching or inquiring faith** in late high school or their early twenties. In this style of faith we search for our own answers to the age-old questions of life, and we sort out just what we believe. It is a time of asking, "Is this really what I believe, or am I just accepting it because someone told me to believe it?" Some people never feel comfortable inquiring into their beliefs, and some people give up on faith when they begin to question their beliefs. But it is a natural process of maturity. Teachers dealing with youth and adults need to be clarifiers of the faith, lifting up dilemmas, encouraging thought, and being open to many viewpoints. Role play (acting out what you would do in a given situation) and open-ended stories (asking the student to finish the story) are good clarifying experiences.

☐ List ways that you can enable your students to inquire into their faith:

_____

_____

_____

_____

Owned Faith

☐ Write the name of a person who you believe exemplifies a mature faith. It may even be someone whom you don't know personally. Write something about how that person exhibits his or her faith.

_____

_____

_____

_____

After we have had the opportunity to inquire into our faith, we can move to an **owned faith.** We then own and acknowledge our beliefs, witness in word and action, and feel comfortable sharing our beliefs with others. At the same time, someone in an owned style of faith is not threatened by others whose beliefs may differ and remains open to hearing other views while searching.

☐ List some ways that you can expose your students to persons who are mature in their faith. Who might those persons be?

_____

_____

_____

_____

31

The Whole View

An oak seedling, in a tree's first year of growth, is as much an oak tree as a hundred-year-old oak. Likewise, we must recognize that a person who operates in the experiential or affiliated style of faith has a legitimate faith.

Sometimes we become stunted in our growth at one stage or another. But as a tree cannot live if we cut out some of its rings, we also must use all our styles of faith throughout our lives. We never lose our need to experience God. To keep our faith fresh, we always need those relationships with other Christians. And we can never say, "I've already inquired about that belief, and so I don't want to think about it again." Once we stop inquiring, we begin to die, like a rotted tree.

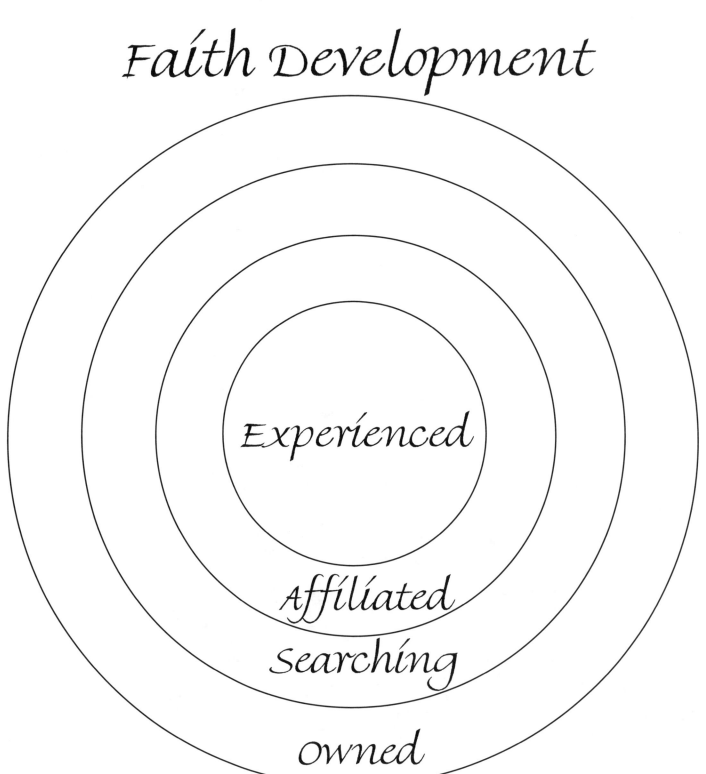

Faith Development

Experienced

Affiliated

Searching

Owned

Additional Studies

James Fowler, a professor at Candler School of Theology (Emory University, Atlanta), has made a great contribution to the study of faith development with his book *Stages of Faith*.[1] In the book Fowler suggests seven stages of faith. The stages are general and may vary with different persons.

Primal Faith—Pre-language disposition of trust and loyalty. Rituals and caregiving are dominant. *(birth through two years of age)*

Intuitive-Projective Faith—Learning by imitating with rapid imaginative development even before the child can distinguish clearly between imagination and reality. *(ages three to seven)*

Mythic-Literal—A time in the child's life when everything is literal. Children absorb stories of our faith, but their abstract thinking is still forming. *(elementary age)*

Synthetic-Conventional Faith—Forming their own identity, all parts of the student's world are pulled together. It is important for biblical meaning to relate to real life. *(adolescence)*

Individuative-Reflective Faith—Taking responsibility for personal commitment and beliefs, the student looks at distinctions between varying beliefs, questions meanings, and makes decisions. *(begins late teens or early twenties)*

Conjunctive Faith—Pulling decisions together, unifying personal faith.

Universalizing Faith—Totally immersed in God, yet seeing universal life as a whole.

☐ How do Fowler's faith stages coincide with Westerhoff's? Write your thoughts here.

☐ Into what areas of faith do your students fall? (Be specific about those that fall into one area and others that fall into another.)

Vertical or Horizontal Faith

The Search Institute, in their 1990 report on faith maturity research, charts faith maturity in vertical (relationship with God) and horizontal (relationships with other people) dimensions.[2]

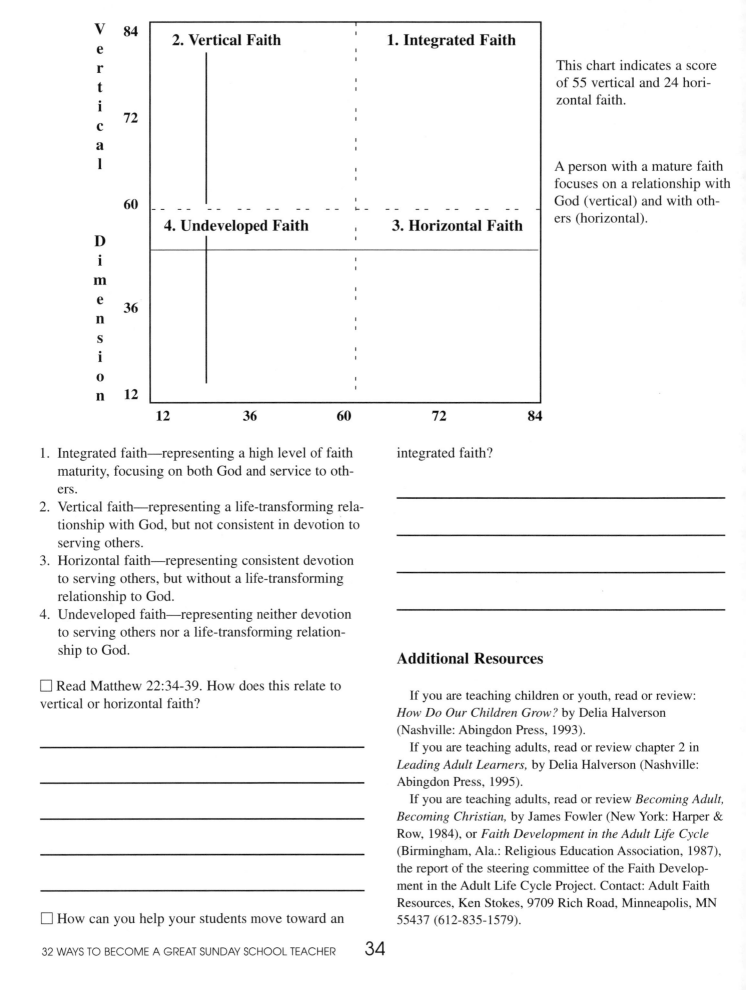

This chart indicates a score of 55 vertical and 24 horizontal faith.

A person with a mature faith focuses on a relationship with God (vertical) and with others (horizontal).

1. Integrated faith—representing a high level of faith maturity, focusing on both God and service to others.
2. Vertical faith—representing a life-transforming relationship with God, but not consistent in devotion to serving others.
3. Horizontal faith—representing consistent devotion to serving others, but without a life-transforming relationship to God.
4. Undeveloped faith—representing neither devotion to serving others nor a life-transforming relationship to God.

☐ Read Matthew 22:34-39. How does this relate to vertical or horizontal faith?

_____

_____

_____

_____

☐ How can you help your students move toward an integrated faith?

_____

_____

_____

_____

Additional Resources

If you are teaching children or youth, read or review: *How Do Our Children Grow?* by Delia Halverson (Nashville: Abingdon Press, 1993).

If you are teaching adults, read or review chapter 2 in *Leading Adult Learners,* by Delia Halverson (Nashville: Abingdon Press, 1995).

If you are teaching adults, read or review *Becoming Adult, Becoming Christian,* by James Fowler (New York: Harper & Row, 1984), or *Faith Development in the Adult Life Cycle* (Birmingham, Ala.: Religious Education Association, 1987), the report of the steering committee of the Faith Development in the Adult Life Cycle Project. Contact: Adult Faith Resources, Ken Stokes, 9709 Rich Road, Minneapolis, MN 55437 (612-835-1579).

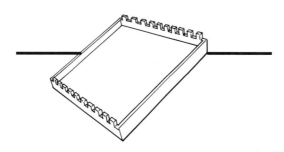

3 How to Read and Study a Bible Passage

Purpose: To refresh your knowledge of the Bible and gain new direction in studying the scripture.

Imagine yourself around a campfire four thousand years ago. You do not have books to read, but in your community there are storytellers. Think of yourself as a person the age of those whom you teach. You might be a young child, cuddled in an adult's arms. Or you might be an older child or youth, admiring the story-teller who seems to know so much. Or you might be an adult, remembering the stories that have been told over and over, and perhaps even remembering some of the events the stories recount. Out of this heritage grew our understanding of God. Through such experi-ences, those who founded our faith shared with others their encounters with God. What a heritage we have in the Bible! What an impact this book has had on the world! And it all began in the story form that we call "oral tradition."

Background Knowledge

When our early ancestors began to develop writing skills, they used the walls of caves and clay tablets to record their markings. Later, they used tanned leather—vellum and parchment—or papyrus, rolled into scrolls. Although the scrolls and clay tablets were portable, they were not practical. They took up space as the nomadic people moved about, and the weight of

the scrolls would slow them down. Consequently, the people continued to learn the stories by hearing them repeated; those with skills in storytelling passed on the tradition orally. Even when paper was invented and the people had more permanent dwellings, not all the details of a story were usually written down. One sheet of paper usually cost as much as a week's salary, and so it was used carefully. Anything that the reader was expected to know or be familiar with was not includ-ed. If necessary, the storyteller could add those facts during the telling.

☐ Even if you know it by memory, take a few minutes to read slowly Psalm 23. What sort of images would the following verses call to mind if you knew nothing about a sheep or a shepherd?

Verse 1

_____

_____

Verse 2

_____

_____

35

Verse 4

_____

_____

Verse 5

_____

_____

☐ The following information would have been common knowledge at the time of the writing. After reading the information below, go back and read the particular verse again, and then write down ways that your thoughts would be different with the new understanding.

Verse 1: Sheep in the Middle East are never driven, as we see cattle driven. Rather, the sheep know their shepherd and will follow him, even when several herds of sheep have been kept together in a fold.

_____

_____

Verse 2: Sheep will graze grass to the roots if allowed to stay in the same place very long. They will even die of starvation before searching for green pastures. The shepherd must find the new food.

_____

_____

Sheep will not drink from rushing water. They will lie down and die of thirst beside a rushing stream before they will drink from it.

_____

_____

Verse 4: The Hebrew word for "rod" used here indicates a weapon. There were many wild animals that could easily attack a defenseless sheep. Shepherds used the rod to fight them off. The staff was a long

stick with a crook at the end. This was used to reach sheep that were caught in thornbushes or had fallen off the rocks, and gently pull them back to safety.

_____

_____

Verse 5: Among the hills and cliffs of that area there were mesas, or flat "tables" of land, where grass was plentiful and made grazing easy.

_____

_____

Sheep often encountered snakes or biting insects. Their eyes would become infected by flying insects. The oil that the shepherd carried had healing agents in it and it helped to keep insects away.

_____

_____

A "cup" for the sheep was a small rocked-in pond beside the well where water was poured so that the sheep might drink.

_____

_____

At the time the psalms were written, many people who were not Hebrews believed in a god they called Baal. They built altars to Baal on most of the mountains or "high places" in the country. These altars were a constant reminder of the worship of this god.

☐ Now read Psalm 121. Does your version of the Bible use a period or question mark at the end of the first verse? The Hebrew language had absolutely _no_ punctuation. Translators have to decide just what the writer might have meant and then add the punctuation. The King James Version uses a period at the end of the first verse. Later translations take into account what was happening at that time and change it to a question mark.

_____

_____

☐ How does the understanding of these altars to Baal and the use of a question mark change the meaning of this psalm?

_____

_____

_____

_____

All of this background information is helpful in understanding just what the writers of the Bible passages actually meant in their time. This does not mean that we can't, for example, continue to use Psalm 121 as a prayer of thanksgiving for the hills, but it does help us to understand just how strong the writer felt about the worship of God over the worship of false gods.

☐ Find a Bible dictionary and other resources on the background of the Bible and become familiar with them. Spend time reading about Hebrew home life, the marketplace, transportation, marriage laws, foods, and so forth.

Translations

Our Bible is made up of books or writings from various times. The Old Testament books were pretty well established by Jesus' lifetime. They were finally agreed upon at the Jewish Synod of Jamnia in 90 C.E. The material in the New Testament was not written down until well after Jesus' death, because it was expected that Jesus would return right away. Most of the New Testament writings are about Jesus' life, the early church, or letters to persons in the early church. It is believed that the Gospels (Matthew, Mark, Luke, and John) were written between 70 and 100 C.E. There were other writings that told of Jesus' life, and other letters as well. The ones we now have in the New Testament were formally accepted by councils at Laodicea (363 C.E.) and Carthage (397 C.E.), although they had been acknowledged long before that. The scriptures went through many transcriptions by scribes; however, their accuracy was confirmed when, during the winter of 1946–47, manuscripts that were one thousand years older than any others were found in a cave near the Dead Sea. These are known as the Dead Sea Scrolls.

Our translations today stem directly from early Hebrew manuscripts of the Old Testament and Greek manuscripts of the New Testament. Most of the early translations simply revised earlier Latin translations. However, in about 400 C.E. a linguist named Jerome went back to the original Greek and Hebrew for a new Latin translation. It became the accepted translation from which most others were then made (including the King James Version), until the late 1800s. The Revised Standard Version (RSV) used both the originals and the King James Version (KJV). The Jerusalem Bible (JB) in 1966 was the first English translation to rely only on the original Hebrew and Greek manuscripts. Most translators today work from the originals, including the Dead Sea Scrolls. The New Revised Standard Version (NRSV) is considered quite accurate.

The King James Version was written during Shakespeare's time, using the common terms of the day. If you enjoy reading Shakespeare you will probably enjoy that version. One example is the use of the pronouns "thee" and "thou." These were originally very personal pronouns, reserved for close friends and members of the family. "You" and "your" were reserved for formal speech and royalty. Today's English completely changes this usage. Translations such as Today's English Version (GNB), also known as the Good News Bible, use words that younger generations feel more comfortable with today.

There have also been paraphrases of the Bible. These are not direct translations but try to keep the same context and meaning while rephrasing the sentences in more understandable words. The most popular of these is The Living Bible. J. B. Phillips wrote a popular paraphrase of the New Testament in the early fifties that is still relevant today.

When seriously studying scripture, it is beneficial to read the same reference from several translations. However, it is less confusing for children if we select and use the same translation that is found in their printed curriculum.

Verses and Chapters

There were originally no paragraphs or chapter and verse markings in the Bible. Nowadays we refer to scripture by writing the name of the book first with the chapter following it. Then we add a colon and put the verse (or verses) after that. A short dash between verses indicates that all verses between are included. If separate verses are used in the same chapter, a comma divides them. If additional chapters from the same book are used, a semicolon divides them.

☐ Read Colossians 3:20–4:1-6. Where is the natural break in these verses?

_____

_____

_____

The chapter break comes after verse 25 of chapter 3; however, recent scholars place verse 4:1 with the preceding verses and begin a new paragraph with verse 2 (notice that 4:1 deals with relationships between persons; 4:2 begins the subject of prayer). Chapter and verse breaks are helpful, if not always precise, for grouping subject matter.

Methods of Study

There are probably as many methods of Bible study as there are study groups using the Bible. You may already have one that best fits your needs. Sometimes, however, we receive new insights by using various methods. Select a passage and try these suggestions. Be sure that you read the passage in *context,* reading what went on before and after the selected part.

☐ Most Bibles have *introductory paragraphs* about each separate book. Read the introductory information and then, as you read the passage, try to imagine yourself as the reader, in that particular time, place, and circumstance.

☐ *Paraphrase* the passage. To do this, read the scripture and then allow yourself a few minutes to think about it. Then write the message, rewording it with your own words.

☐ Try *journaling* along with your study. After you have read the scripture, spend some time in prayer and then write down any thoughts that come to your mind as you are inspired by the passage.

_____

_____

_____

☐ Use *study Bibles* for ideas of how the scripture has spoken to other people. Recognize, however, that although those who write these study helps in the Bible have done a great deal of study themselves, they bring their own background and understanding to the scriptures. Use their helps, but don't worry if you disagree with them from time to time. This is a part of your own inquiring faith development.

☐ *Use your senses* as you read the following passages.

—Imagine the *sound* of rustling grain as you "walk" through the fields with Jesus and the disciples (Matt. 12:1-8).
—*Feel* the hunger of a person in the multitude that Jesus fed (John 6:1-15).
—*Weep* with Mary and Martha at Lazarus' death (John 11:1-44). Jesus wept with them even though he knew he was going to raise Lazarus from the dead.
—*Visualize* the Sea of Galilee and *smell* the fishing nets (Luke 5:1-11).
—*Taste* the fresh fish that Jesus cooked on the grill (John 21:1-14).
—*Feel* the grit on the disciples' feet after walking on dusty roads, and appreciate the refreshing coolness as Jesus washed their feet (John 13:1-17).

☐ Use the *depth Bible study* that is suggested by Dick Murray in his book *Teaching the Bible to Adults and Youth,* pages 35-39. First read the passage straight through. Then answer the following questions:

What does the text actually say? What happened? Who did what?

_____

_____

_____

What meaning can this passage have for us (our church or community or nation) today? Consider what elements in the story are different from the situation today.

_____

_____

_____

_____

What does the passage mean to me personally, as an individual?

_____

_____

_____

What does this passage say to us about the relationship between God and human beings?

_____

_____

_____

_____

_____

Are there other Christian concepts that this passage tells us about?

_____

_____

_____

No matter what method of Bible study you may use, take into account the "Principles of Bible Study" that follow. These are particularly helpful if you are working in a group Bible study.

Principles of Bible Study

1. God's Word is Jesus Christ.	*We look behind, in, and through words of the Bible for God's Word (Jesus Christ).*
2. No Christian has a monopoly on understanding.	*We all listen to one another as we seek to understand.*
3. Assume everyone has Christian integrity.	*We'll not accuse one another of being unchristian.*
4. Assume we will reach different understandings.	*We are more disturbed with this than God is.*
5. Few know Hebrew or Greek.	*We should use various English versions.*
6. Accept differences among us.	*These differences are important and do matter.*
7. We may end up with different biblical understandings.	*We can still be warm Christian friends.*[1]

☐ Try the *theological study* also suggested by Dick Murray (pages 40-44). Read the passage straight through, and then answer these questions:

What does this passage say to us about God?

_____

_____

_____

What does this passage say to us about women and men?

_____

_____

_____

Study Tools

There is a wealth of resources that can help us with our understanding of the Bible. If you do not have the following suggested items, borrow them from your church library or a public library. You may also be able to borrow them from your pastor.

☐ *Introductory materials* in the front of your Bible will give you insight into how to use your particular Bible. Read the introductory materials and note anything new that you learn.

_____

_____

☐ Many Bibles will have *translators' footnotes* and *cross-reference systems*. The footnotes may give you some insight into the particular times, or they may state that the original words are ambiguous. The cross-reference will guide you to other scriptures that will make that passage more meaningful. Sometimes the cross-references are at the bottom with footnotes, and sometimes they are near the reference in a center column or in the outside margins.

☐ Find any footnotes on Jesus' birth in your Bible and read them. (Matthew 1 and 2 and Luke 1–2:20. Note that Mark and John do not record the birth narratives.) What new insights did you gain?

_____

_____

_____

_____

☐ Find the cross-references suggested for Matthew 5:43 and Luke 8:10. What insights do you gain here?

_____

_____

_____

_____

Look up the following in a *Bible dictionary* and write down interesting information that you find about each.

☐ Look up *money* or *currency* and find out how much the widow's mite would have been worth.

_____

_____

_____

☐ Look up *marriage* and record some differences between that time and today.

_____

_____

☐ Look up *Passover* for background information on the celebration that Jesus shared with his disciples at their last meal before his death. Note what you find here.

_____

_____

_____

☐ Using maps from your Bible or from a *Bible atlas*, trace Paul's route for his second journey: Antioch,

which stories are told in only one Gospel?

Story	Gospel
_____	_____
_____	_____
_____	_____
_____	_____

Lystra, Iconium, Pisidian Antioch, Troas, Neapolis, Philippi, Amphipolis, Apollonia, Thessalonia, Beroea, Cenchrea, Ephesus, and Caesarea.

☐ A *concordance* is a listing of words in the Bible. A complete concordance can have more than two thousand pages. The concordance is written as a companion to a specific translation. Some Bibles contain abbreviated concordances. Use a concordance to look up "feet," and find the reference to Jesus' washing the disciples' feet in the Upper Room:

_____

_____

_____

☐ Use several *Bible commentaries* to look at other people's comments on the following and see how they differ.

Paul's "thorn in the flesh" in 2 Corinthians 12:5-10.

_____

_____

_____

Paul's comments of relationships between men and women in 1 Corinthians 7:4-5, 11:11, 14:26-39; Galatians 3:28.

_____

_____

_____

☐ Using a *Gospel parallel,* where the first three Gospels are printed side by side, look up the following stories. How do they differ in each Gospel?

Cleansing of the Temple (Matt. 21:12-13; Mark 11:15-19; Luke 19:45-48)

_____

_____

_____

The empty tomb (Matt. 28:1-10; Mark 16:1-8; Luke 24:1-11)

_____

_____

Additional Resources

Ball-Kilbourne, Gary. *Get Acquainted with Your Bible* (student and leader guide). Nashville: Abingdon Press, 1993.

Barclay, William. *Introducing the Bible.* Nashville: Abingdon Press, n.d.

————. *The Daily Study Bible Series.* Philadelphia: Westminster Press, 1953–59.

Beasley, James, et al. *An Introduction to the Bible.* Nashville: Abingdon Press, 1991.

Johnson, Dan. *Neglected Treasure.* Anderson, Ind.: Bristol Books, 1989.

Moore, James. *When All Else Fails, Read the Instructions.* Nashville: Abingdon Press/Dimensions for Living, 1993.

Wright, Chris. *User's Guide to the Bible.* Batavia, Ill.: Lion.

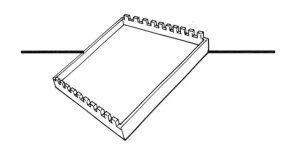

4 Multiple Intelligence Learning

Purpose: To recognize our various gifts of learning and plan for ways to use them in the classroom.

We are created in God's image. God also made each person an individual, with our own unique physical characteristics and our own gifts of learning. At times, during our childhood, specific gifts of learning are developed more fully than others. If we do not have an opportunity to learn in various ways, then some gifts or ways of learning may be blocked. These ways of learning have been categorized into seven distinct areas called *multiple intelligences.* The seven multiple intelligences are: *verbal-linguistic, logical-mathematical, visual-spatial, body-kinesthetic, musical-rhythmic, interpersonal,* and *intrapersonal.*

For years Christian educators have recognized that we do not all learn in the same manner. Much of our ability to live out the Christian teachings rests on our ability to evaluate situations in our world and solve problems associated with those situations.

Howard Gardner is an authority on the multiple intelligences God has given each of us. In actuality, each person uses several of these intelligences as we learn, but sometimes we rely on one or two more heavily than others. Thanks to research on the human brain by Gardner and others in the field, we now have confirmation of our various intelligences. If we can understand these seven ways of learning we are better able to pass our faith on to others.

☐ Recall various methods that were used in your learning as a child. (Examples: writing, memory, ques-

tions and answers, alphabetization, field trips, etc.)

_____

_____

_____

☐ Are there teaching methods that you find difficult to understand when you are learning?

_____

_____

_____

☐ What methods of learning come easiest to you?

_____

_____

_____

_____

☐ What methods of learning seem the hardest?

_____

_____

_____

_____

Verbal-Linguistic

Before written records, the scriptures were shared using what we call the *oral tradition.* Through story-telling, the message of God was passed from generation to generation long before writing was common. Even today, we most often teach using language and words, both written and spoken.

☐ Jesus approached his listeners using verbal-linguistic teaching skills. Sometimes he combined this with visual images in stories. Read Matthew 5:1-12 and Mark 1:21-22.

☐ How have you used verbal-linguistic teaching in the classroom or in other situations?

_____

_____

_____

When verbal-linguistic learning is used alone, it is usually the *least* effective method of teaching.

Logical-Mathematical

When we gear our teaching to this intelligence, we encourage inductive thinking and reasoning, logic, statistics, and abstract patterns.

☐ Jesus used questions and answers to reach his listeners who learned in this manner. Read Luke 22.

☐ Some questions demand a specific answer, but questions that stimulate logical thinking help the logical-mathematical learner. Such questions can begin with: How do you

suppose _____ felt when _____?
or

What do you think would happen if _____?

☐ Write several questions about the good Samaritan that would require logical thought.

_____

_____

_____

_____

☐ What sort of statistic comparing a familiar local distance with the Nazareth-to-Bethlehem route might you use? How would this help a learner grasp the hardships that Mary and Joseph might have faced on their journey?

_____

_____

☐ In what Bible story might you use a time line with older children, youth, and adults?

_____

_____

Visual-Spatial

Although the first two intelligences are most often used in teaching, many people learn best through the use of other intelligences. If we are to reach all of our students, then we must use a variety of methods.

The visual-spatial person responds to visualizing objects and by creating internal mental pictures.

☐ Read Luke 6:47-49; Matthew 13:1-9.

43

☐ What common objects did Jesus use to explain his meanings to persons who learn in this manner?

_____

_____

_____

_____

☐ Find a quiet place and read the following, using the suggestions to visualize your prayer and pausing to reflect between paragraphs.

> Sit quietly and close your eyes for a moment, breathing in and out slowly. Breathe in through your nose deeply, feeling your breath come from your feet all the way up to your head. Then breathe out through your mouth.
>
> Imagine that you are at a special place that you like to go to alone. It might be outside, or somewhere in your house. In your thoughts, look around this special place and remember what makes it special.
>
> Think about the part of yourself that laughs when you are happy and cries when you are sad, the part that loves and feels great when you do something for someone else. Some people might call this our *soul.*
>
> Invite God into this central part of yourself, into your soul. Tell God about a problem you have. It may be a problem concerning another person, or a decision you need to make, or something else that is troubling you.
>
> Ask God's help in dealing with the problem. Explain to God that it's more than you can deal with by yourself, and then give it to God.
>
> Know that God is loving you, even while you are experiencing problems. Remember, Jesus did not say that life would be easy, only that he would be with us. Feel God's love surround you as you sit quietly for a few moments.
>
> Arise, refreshed, knowing that God will help you handle the situation. You may not have the answer now, but know that it will come.

☐ Record some of the thoughts and feelings you experienced during this prayer.

_____

_____

_____

_____

☐ How might you use a visualized prayer with your class?

_____

_____

_____

_____

Body-Kinesthetic

How often have you nibbled on popcorn or some other snack while you studied? Perhaps you find yourself tapping your foot to music as you read. The body-kinesthetic intelligence relates to the physical body, such as movement and physical activity.

☐ Read John 13:1-17. What physical activity did Jesus use to teach something here?

_____

_____

_____

☐ In what ways have you, or a teacher you know, used movement in teaching?

_____

_____

what Intelligence?

In the list of teaching methods below, use the key to identify which intelligences are used in the following teaching methods. Some methods will use several intelligences.

KEY

V/L Visual-Linguistic
L/M Logical-Mathematical
V/S Visual-Spatial
B/K Body-Kinesthetic
M/R Musical-Rhythmic
Inter Interpersonal
Intra Intrapersonal

_____Storytelling

_____Silent prayer

_____Finger painting

_____Mobiles

_____Singing prayers

_____Rap

_____Puzzles

_____Musical instruments

_____Cooking

_____Nature walk

_____Painting, murals, etc.

_____News interviews

_____Maps

_____Time line

_____Collecting

_____Felt board

_____Conversation-Discuss

_____Singing games

_____Board games

_____Collage

_____Video-Film

_____Litany

_____Rhythm sticks

_____Create poems

_____Silent prayer

_____Role play

_____Pantomime

_____Pottery

_____Puppets

_____Research

_____Storytelling

_____Making exhibits

_____Diorama

_____Field trips

Musical-Rhythmic

This intelligence involves recognition of patterns, both tonal and rhythmic.

☐ What are some things that you learned as a child, using music or rhythm (such as the alphabet, scripture, etc.)?

_____

_____

_____

_____

_____

☐ Singing hymns was a part of the common experience of Jesus and his disciples. Read Matthew 26:30.

☐ Borrow a hymnal from your church and look at the scripture index in the back. Turn to several hymns and sing them. List below several hymns that use words from a specific scripture that you like.

_____

_____

_____

_____

Interpersonal

We were created to be in relationship with one another. Most of us, particularly at certain times in our lives, enjoy learning in groups and in relationships with other persons. This intelligence helps us to build better communication skills.

☐ Read John 4:1-30; Mark 6:7-19. Jesus worked with persons on a personal level and also developed small groups, his most successful being the twelve disciples.

☐ If there are twelve persons in a class and each person takes two minutes to respond to a question, how much time will this take? _____ If those same persons were divided into four groups and asked to share their responses within their groups, how much time would this take? _____

Small groups like these offer everyone an opportunity to share. After small-group discussion, you may choose whether or not to have each group report their discussion to the entire class. Your time restraints may determine this. Don't worry about knowing what each group discusses, since they will learn as they wrestle with the discussion.

Intrapersonal

Through self-reflection and awareness of the spirit within us, we can find God's direction. Many times the Bible mentions Jesus drawing away from everyone for solitude or taking his disciples away for a period of reflection.

☐ Read Matthew 14:13-23 and Mark 14:32-36.

☐ How can you encourage intrapersonal learning experiences for your class?

_____

_____

_____

_____

_____

Additional Resources

Bruce, Barbara. *7 Ways of Teaching the Bible to Children.* Nashville: Abingdon Press, 1996.

Gardner, Howard. *Frames of Mind: The Theory of Multiple Intelligences.* New York: Harper and Row, 1983.

Lazear, David. *Seven Ways of Knowing.* Palatino, Ill.: IRI/Skylight Publishing, 1991.

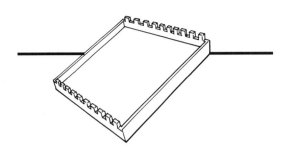

5 why christian Education?

Purpose: To explore the origins and reasons for teaching our faith and firmly state what you hope will happen to the students through your teaching.

In biblical times the foundational faith tenets were passed to the children in the home. As the Christian faith developed, formal faith education for the general population was limited to the preparation time spent before becoming a part of the fellowship of believers. In the late 1700s, the Sunday school began in England and spread rapidly across America.

However, Christian education is more than a Sunday morning class. It can happen anywhere, and it extends into the home. It happens when Christians gather for a celebration. It happens when two persons talk together about a life problem and when someone models a Christian action.

In 1990, a study of 561 randomly chosen congregations in six prominent denominations was released by Search Institute under the title *Effective Christian Education: A National Study of Protestant Congregations.*[1]

Several findings came from that study. The study indicated that youths and adults with the strongest maturity in faith had experienced lifetime involvement in an effective Christian education program. The study indicated that Christian education is strengthened through nurturing a thinking climate, building a caring community, and involving people in service to others.

The research also identified these traits of effective teachers, whether they teach in a regular Sunday school program or in some other way:

- A willingness to grow and learn along with those whom they teach.
- A knowledge of their students—their likes and dislikes, their joys and sorrows.
- A knowledge of how people learn and grow through life stages.
- A faith that is seen not only in words they speak, but in their actions in the congregation and the larger community.
- A growing knowledge of the Bible and a willingness to continue studying and pondering the scriptures.
- A teaching style that invites others into the learning situation and awakes in them a desire to know God as they see God known by their teacher.

When I ask a group of adults what they remember most about their childhood Sunday school experience, they seldom mention a specific thing that they were taught. Instead, they tell me about a teacher and how that teacher exemplified Christ.

Just Why Is It Important?

Evidently you believe that education is an important part of the church, or you would not be working on this study. But just why is it necessary? How would you rank the reasons for teaching in the church that follow?

☐ First read through the following statements. Add additional statements if you like.

☐ Now, considering number 1 as most important, use a scale from 1 to 10 to rank each statement according to its importance.

☐ Now, go back through the list and think in depth about each statement. How do they differ? For example, how does learning *about* the Bible differ from learning how to *use* the Bible as a basis for our lives? Make notations of your thoughts.

_____

_____

☐ Study your church and education committee mission statements. How do the reasons for teaching fit into the mission statements?

_____

_____

_____

Through Our Teaching We Seek:

_____ To help persons learn more about the Bible.
_____ To help persons discover that God is active in our world.
_____ To help persons appreciate their faith heritage through the centuries.
_____ To help persons recognize their gifts and develop ways to use them for God and for others.
_____ To help persons know the stories and teachings of Christ.
_____ To help persons respond to the Holy Spirit in their lives.
_____ To help persons use Christian values as they make decisions.
_____ To help persons share the ways that God is active in their lives.
_____ To help persons commune with God.
_____ To help persons recognize ways that God works through them.
_____ To help persons use the Bible as a base for their life.
_____ To help persons see learning to live our faith as a lifelong venture.
_____ To help persons become active in the family of God by building relationships and working together with others.
_____ To help persons show their faith to others through their actions.
_____ To help persons become aware of the needs of other people around the world and in their own communities.
_____ To help persons learn to settle disputes peacefully.
_____ To help persons recognize the worth of all people, no matter what their race, nationality, abilities, or beliefs.

_____

_____

_____

☐ Read Deuteronomy 4:9-10; 6:1-9; 31:12; and Matthew 28:19-20. What did these mandates say to the people of that time?

_____

_____

_____

_____

_____

☐ What do these mandates say to you, as you consider teaching?

_____

_____

_____

_____

_____

☐ Sit in silence for a few moments and reflect on the reasons for teaching and on the scriptures. Listen to what God may be telling you now.

☐ Using the form on page 49, prayerfully write your own statements for what you hope will happen to people whom you teach.

My challenge in Teaching

- To help persons _____.

- To help persons _____.

- To help persons _____.

- To help persons _____.

- To help persons _____.

- To help persons _____.

- To help persons _____.

- To help persons _____.

- To help persons _____.

- To help persons _____.

- To help persons _____.

Signed _____

Additional Resources

Foster, Charles R. *Educating Congregations.* Nashville: Abingdon Press, 1994.

Foundations: Shaping the Ministry of Christian Education in Your Congregation. Nashville: Discipleship Resources, 1993 (esp. chaps. 1 and 2).

Roehlkepartain, Eugene C. *The Teaching Church.* Nashville: Abingdon Press, 1993.

THE WARP: PERSONAL ENRICHMENT

6 Enriching My Prayer Life

Purpose: To better understand prayer and make it a more eminent pa[rt] of your life.

Prayer is like coming to God as Moses did, removing our shoes because we recognize that we are in God's presence. Moses also spoke to God in a personal way, even putting up arguments for why he should not be the one to approach Pharaoh. Prayer is a very natural event. We were created with the need to communicate, in fact, for the *purpose* of communication with God. The simplest way to explain prayer is to refer to it as talking with and listening to God.

Prayer is not just another duty that we must add to our already crowded schedule. If that were so, most of us would never have time to pray! Praying may be a very simple act. Think of a child's prayer. A prayer can be as simple as rejoicing in the fresh grass after a rain and thinking or saying, "Thank you, God, for the refreshing rain." It doesn't have to be a deep emotional experience.

As our relationship with God deepens, we learn to live our prayers, simply living our life by asking for God's guidance. Each action can be prayer if we turn it toward God.

Jesus' Prayer Life

☐ Locate and read Mark 1:29-34.

Close your eyes and imagine Jesus in a home with a crowd of people pressing all around him, demanding that he heal them. Feel the closeness, the lack of air circulating, and the drain of energy.

☐ Write how you felt after reading Mark 1:29-34.

_____

_____

_____

_____

_____

☐ Read Mark 1:35. Close your eyes and imagine the release Jesus must have felt as he talked with God, away from the crowds.

☐ Write how you felt.

_____

_____

_____

_____

☐ Look up additional times that Jesus prayed, using the following list of scriptures and form.

Matt. 6:9b-13	Mark 1:35	Luke 5:15-16	John 11:41b-42
Matt. 14:18-21	Mark 14:36	Luke 6:12-16	John 12:27-28
Matt. 14:22-23	Mark 15:34	Luke 9:28-29	John 17
Matt. 19:13-14		Luke 10:21b-22	John 21:13
Matt. 26:26-29		Luke 23:34	
Matt. 26:36-43		Luke 23:46	
		Luke 24:30	
		Luke 24:50-51	

Scripture: _____

*W*hat was happening before Jesus prayed? _____

_____

*W*hen did Jesus pray? _____

_____

*W*here was Jesus when he prayed? _____

_____

*W*ho was with Jesus when he prayed? _____

_____

*W*hat kind of prayer did Jesus pray? _____

_____

*W*hy do you think Jesus felt the need to pray? _____

_____

ENRICHING MY PRAYER LIFE

☐ List the times and settings when we pray today, both alone and with others, dividing the settings into three categories:

Private	Small Group	Corporate (Large Group)
_____	_____	_____
_____	_____	_____
_____	_____	_____
_____	_____	_____
_____	_____	_____

Like a three-legged stool that needs all its legs the same length, it is important that we have a balance of all three prayer situations.

The ACTS of Prayer

By using the word *ACTS*, we can remember the four important elements in our prayer life.

A doration
C onfession
T hanksgiving
S upplication

☐ On the left, list all the reasons that you love God.

I love God because:

_____

_____

_____

_____

_____

I love God

Now, cover up the listing on the left side, and think about loving God, not for a reason, but simply because you *love!* That is adoration.

From the earliest of biblical times, there are references to the "fear of God." For biblical people, this phrase did not hold the same meaning that we connect with the word *fear* today. It was used when the writer was speaking of the "awe" of God.

However, **adoration** is even more than that. We can be in awe of the power of the split atom, but that awe does not cause us to worship it or to look to that power for strength and help. There must be a personal relationship in adoration. It is more like the simple term "looking and loving." We look to God, admiring what God has done for us and in awe of all of God's power, yet there is a personal loving that goes out from us in response to the personal love that we feel from God.

In **confession** we meet God and accept the whole truth about ourselves. Confession is difficult without having experienced adoration. When we accept the love God gives us, and we experience our love for God that adoration brings, then we feel confident in opening and revealing our whole self to God.

☐ List acts that separate you from God.

_____

_____

_____

_____

_____

One definition for sin is our separation from God. If an act separates us from God, then it is something that we need to confess in order to right our relationship with God. Often we get hung up on particular "sins" when actually these are only symptoms of the real sin, the real thing that separates us from God. An example of this might be anger. Anger in itself is only a feeling, and neither right nor wrong. However, an attitude that we may have that causes anger, or the way that we express our anger, may be a sin. Perhaps our attitude is a determination to always have our own way; or perhaps we express our anger by making a sarcastic remark to another person. These are the things that we need to look at in our confession to God.

We can help our students look at *why* they get "mad" and their responsibility in the method they choose to vent their anger, instead of simply telling them that they mustn't get angry. The blanket statement, "I'm sorry," can become trite if we don't dig deeper into what caused our feelings or why we reacted the way we did.

Thanksgiving is an easy type of prayer. Our beginning prayers as small children are usually prayers of thanksgiving. It is always easier to say "Thank you" than to say "I was wrong," or to dig into our sins and say "I am sorry."

Prayers of thanksgiving can be spontaneous as well as planned. You might tell a child, "I thank God for the way that you are playing with your friend." This statement in itself is a type of prayer. Look for thanksgiving opportunities throughout the day. Draw closer to God yourself and help students consider all that they have to be thankful for, including the disappointments and failures that help us grow. With the joy of thanksgiving, we can enter into a creative partnership with God.

Supplication is a word seldom used today. *Petition* is another word for this act of prayer. However, because our petitions of today usually apply pressure for change (the more names on a petition, the more likely we are to get what we want), we can often get the wrong idea about the petitions in a prayer. Pounding away at God does not make for a creative partnership.

The prayer of supplication might be looked at as a sort of senior-junior partnership with God, in which the junior partner recognizes needs and the senior partner is aware of the needs and helps the junior partner to grow in achieving those needs. If the senior partner were simply to meet those needs without the junior partner's conscious efforts, then there would be no growth.

When we identify our needs and petition God, we recognize that God is in control of the world and of our lives. We give our wants and desires over to God, instead of pleading with God to "come over to our side." Prayer is not a matter of playing sides and persuasion, but a matter of creative partnership. Supplication is a loving surrender to God. When we realize that God is in charge, our prayers of supplication will reflect this. God will give us strength and insight to live our lives as effectively as possible.[1]

☐ Read the prayer of supplication that Jesus used in Luke 22:42. What might be included in your own prayer of supplication at this point in your life?

_____

_____

_____

_____

_____

Practicing the Presence

There was a monk, many years ago, who practiced finding God in everyday situations. His name was Brother Lawrence, and the following is from a book about him titled *The Practice of the Presence of God.*

Brother Lawrence insisted that it is necessary to always be aware of God's presence by talking with Him throughout each day. To think that you must abandon conversation with Him in order to deal with the world is erroneous. Instead, as we nourish our souls by seeing God in his exaltation, we will derive a great joy at being His.

The dear brother remarked that we must give ourselves *totally* to God, in both temporal and spiritual affairs. Our only happiness should come from doing God's will, whether it brings us some pain or great pleasure. After all, if we're truly devoted to doing God's will, pain and pleasure won't make any difference to us.

We also need to be faithful, even in dry periods. We should take advantage of those times to practice our determination and our surrender to Him. This will often bring us to a maturity further on in our walk with God.[2]

53

☐ Divide a sheet of paper in half down the middle. On the left, list things that draw you closer to God (include swimming, walking, visiting, etc.). On the right, list things that pull you away from God.

Select one item from the left-hand column. Close your eyes and imagine yourself doing that. In your imaging, think of how you can commune with God as you are doing this particular thing. Write it here:

_____

_____

_____

_____

Select another item from the left-hand column. Again, close your eyes and imagine. How can you commune with God here?

_____

_____

_____

_____

Look at the right-hand column. What changes do you need to make here? Select an item from the right-hand column. Write a one-sentence prayer that you can pray each time you need to ask God to help you with this.

_____

_____

_____

_____

Breath Prayer

Sometimes we have trouble focusing although we really feel a need to pray. Ron DelBene, in his book *When I'm Alone* (pp. 7-9), suggests using a breath prayer. Quite simply, this is a prayer that may be said in one breath, breathing in and out.

☐ Make yourself comfortable and quiet. Close your eyes and remind yourself that God loves you and you are in God's presence. Recall a favorite poem or passage of scripture, such as:

Be still, and know that I am God! (Ps. 46:10)

☐ Imagine that God is calling you by name. Listen carefully and hear God asking,
"_____ [*your name*], what do you want?"

☐ Answer God with whatever comes honestly from your heart. Use one or two words or a short phrase in the answer, such as:
Peace. *or*
I want to feel your forgiveness.

_____

_____

If several ideas come out, combine or focus so that you find a specific need that is as basic to your spiritual well-being as water is to life.

Ask yourself: What do I want that will make me feel most whole? Peace of mind and peace of heart will follow wholeness.

☐ Choose your favorite name for God: God, Jesus, Christ, Lord, Spirit, Creator.

_____

_____

_____

☐ Combine your name for God with your answer to God's question, "What do you want?" This becomes your breath prayer. It may be:

Let me know your peace, O God.
or
Jesus, I need to let go of troubles.

Try placing God's name at the beginning or at the end. One way may feel more comfortable than the other. Change the words as needed so that the sentence flows smoothly, as in a breath.

Now say or think the words of the prayer as you breathe in and breathe out. Write the prayer down and use it several times during the day—in fact, anytime you think about it. Soon it will become a part of your life.[3]

Pray for Students

Unless we pray, we cannot grow. See page 60 for a suggested prayer calendar to use when praying for your students.

PRAYER

P *repare yourself.* Find a location that is comfortable and where you will not be disturbed.

R *epeat a simple verse or prayer.* Learn a short Bible verse or prayer or song. Breathe slowly for several seconds, being conscious of your breathing, and then repeat the verse or prayer or sing the song quietly. You might try 1 Timothy 1:2*b* or a verse from Psalms, perhaps 8:1*a* or 46:10. Or sing "Spirit of the Living God" or pray Brother Lawrence's prayer, "Lord, make me according to Thy heart."

A *ccept God into your heart.* To do this, center into the very heart of you. Consider the part of you that feels love, that feels sadness, the part that is happy when you do for others. Then ask God to come into that part of you.

Y *ield all that bothers you to God.* Whatever is troubling you, turn it over to God. Know that God understands your problems.

E *njoy God's presence.* Just spend some time "looking upon and loving" God. Relax in the joy of being loved by God. Feel God's strength and peace.

R *eview how you felt.* I suggest that you begin a prayer journal, writing down some of the feelings and thoughts that came to you as you prayed. Writing it down makes your feelings and thoughts more concrete.[4]

Praying Regularly

Most of us need to discipline ourselves in order to include a specific time for prayer each day. Surprisingly, when we do take the time to talk with God our day seems to run smoother. If you do not have a routine system in your prayer time, you might want to try this suggestion. Adjust it to your needs, but also feel free to change your method of praying from time to time.

_____

_____

_____

_____

Additional Resources

☐ Locate and review several of these resources. Decide on at least one that you will read in the next month in order to continue to enrich your communication with God.

Broyles, Anne. *Journaling: A Spirit Journey.* Nashville: Upper Room, 1988.

DelBene, Ron. *The Breath of Life.* Nashville: Upper Room, 1992.

———. *When I'm Alone.* Nashville: Upper Room, 1988.

Dunnam, Maxie. *Workbook of Living Prayer.* Nashville: Upper Room, 1975.

Foster, Richard. *Prayer.* San Francisco: HarperCollins, 1992.

Halverson, Delia. *Living Simply.* Nashville: Abingdon Press, 1996.

Olsen, Charles. *Transforming Church Boards into Communities of Spiritual Leaders.* Bethesda, Md.: Alban Institute, 1995.

Webb, Lance. *The Art of Personal Prayer* (Abingdon Classics). Nashville: Abingdon Press, 1992.

ENRICHING MY PRAYER LIFE

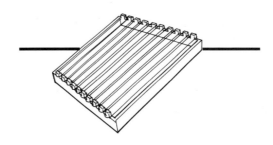

7 our Faith Story in the Bible

Purpose: To recognize how our understanding of God has developed down through the years and appreciate our heritage of witnesses.

Our heritage of witnessing as storytellers, faith-sharers, and God-sharers goes back for centuries and centuries. Think about the persons who went before us as witnesses to the story, a part of our heritage.

A Line of Witnesses

This is the story of people, of people whom God made. And it is the story of the sort of understanding that those people had, and have, of their relationship with their Creator.

God found a man in the city of Haran. The man often talked with God, and God was very special to the man. God chose that man and told him to take his wife and go to a foreign land. Although the man was old, God told him that he and his wife would have a child and that from that child God would bring a great nation. God promised to be their God and that they would be God's people. The people were called Hebrews.

The man is a witness to the story—a part of our heritage. The name of that man was *Abraham,* and the name of his wife was *Sarah.* The name of their son was *Isaac.*

☐ Read the account of Abraham and Sarah in Genesis 12–21 (particularly Gen. 12:1-6; 17:1-8, 15-19; 21:1-7). Reflect on the people's understanding of God.

_____

_____

_____

_____

_____

_____

AND THE STORY GOES ON—

Isaac had sons, and his sons had sons. Sibling rivalry was as common then as it is now. All down the line, brothers squabbled. Although God did not approve of the hatred, God was able to use the results of this hatred for good. Through one brother who was sold to traveling merchants, God helped the Hebrew people move to Egypt and avoid a terrible famine that was in their land.

That man is a witness to the story—a part of our heritage. And the name of the brother who was sold into Egypt was *Joseph.*

☐ Read the account of Joseph's life from Genesis 37 through 47 (particularly Gen. 37; 41; 42:1-3; 43:1-2; 45:4-15). Reflect on the people's understanding of God.

_____

_____

_____

_____

_____

_____

AND THE STORY GOES ON—

Many years passed, and the people lived in Egypt and did well. But then came a new ruler who did not know Joseph, so the people were treated harshly. They became slaves, and things did not go well. When things did not go well, the people soon forgot that God was with them. They felt that their God was as distant as the gods that the people around them worshiped.

In the midst of their hard times, a baby was born. The ruler of the land had declared that each Hebrew boy baby should be killed. And so the baby's mother hid the baby in a stream where she knew the ruler's daughter would find him. The ruler's daughter did find him and raised him as her own. But the boy grew up and knew that the Hebrews were his people, and he killed a man who was beating one of his people. He became afraid and ran away.

After many years of work in a foreign land, he had a personal experience with God that changed his life. He received a call to help God deliver the Hebrews. But he did not think that his people would believe he had experienced such a personal encounter with God. They no longer believed that God spoke to people. And so he asked for a sign for his people, as well as signs for the ruler of the country. **That man is a witness to the story—a part of our heritage.** That man was *Moses.* And he had a brother who helped him, named Aaron.

☐ Read the early stories of Moses in Exodus 2 through 13. Reflect on the people's understanding of God.

_____

_____

_____

_____

_____

_____

_____

AND THE STORY GOES ON—

There was a woman at that time who had watched over Moses when his mother hid him in the river. She was his sister, and she later helped Moses with his mission. **That woman is a witness to the story—a part of our heritage.** Her name was *Miriam.*

☐ Reread Genesis 2:1-8 and read Exodus 15:1-21. Reflect on the people's understanding of God.

_____

_____

_____

_____

_____

_____

_____

AND THE STORY GOES ON—

Now Moses did follow his calling, and he and Miriam, with their brother Aaron's assistance, did help the people to escape. There were many signs that God loved the people and that God wanted to be personally involved with the people.

☐ Read Exodus 13:20-21; 14:5-31; 15:22-25; 16:1-36; 17:1-7. Reflect on the people's understanding of God.

_____

_____

OUR FAITH STORY IN THE BIBLE

_____

_____

_____

But the people just couldn't believe it. The people had been out of contact with God for so long that they could not grasp the idea that God would guide each one of them in everything they did.

And so the people asked for something more concrete, something that they could *see*. They still needed a crutch on which to lean. God gave them two stone tablets with ten laws to guide them. You can't get much more concrete than stone! If they had only learned to live close to God and to follow God personally in everything they did, they would not have needed specific laws.

☐ Read Exodus 20:1-21; 24:12-18; and chapters 32 through 34. Reflect on how the people changed their understanding of God.

_____

_____

_____

_____

AND THE STORY GOES ON—

Some years later there was a woman in another country, married to a Hebrew. This woman had learned of God's love from her husband and her mother-in-law. She accepted God's love, and when her husband died she left her own country to travel with her mother-in-law to her home country. She told her mother-in-law, "Where you go, I will go. . . . Your people shall be my people, and your God my God." **That woman is a witness to the story—a part of our heritage.** And the name of that woman was *Ruth.*

☐ Read the book of Ruth. Reflect on Naomi and Ruth's understanding of God.

_____

_____

_____

AND THE STORY GOES ON—

Even the ten laws were not enough. The people had to have a place in which to keep the ten laws, and so they built an ark, and then they later built a temple to house the ark. And soon they centered their worship on physical crutches: the ten laws, the ark, and the temple.

The time came when another nation captured the Hebrews and took them into a foreign land. The people had connected God with their holy city, Jerusalem, and the Temple for so long that they did not believe that God could be with them in a foreign land.

God sent prophets to remind them, and some of the people built synagogues in which to worship. But after they returned to their own land they rebuilt the temple and began relying on intricate interpretations of the ten laws to get them through their days. The laws became their god instead of the one true God. They centered their minds and hearts on the ten laws instead of on their true God.

☐ Read 2 Chronicles 36:15-23; Ezra 1; 3; Isaiah 9:1-7; 11:1-2. Reflect on the warning of the prophets.

_____

_____

_____

_____

AND THE STORY GOES ON—

Finally God came to the people in a way that they could understand. God became flesh and dwelt among them. And then the people—at least some of the people—understood. **That man is a witness to the story—a part of our heritage.** In fact, he is the main witness and the main part of the story. That man, who was "God with skin on," was *Jesus.*

☐ Read Luke 4:14-37; Mark 10:13-16; Luke 15:11-32; Matthew 23:37-39. Reflect on how Jesus changed the people's understanding of God.

_____

_____

_____

_____

_____

AND THE STORY GOES ON—

Jesus chose to train twelve men. One of those men earned his living catching fish. His faith was strong when things went well, but when the going got rough he became anxious. He even denied Jesus three times when Jesus was in trouble. But Jesus knew that this fisherman could become a firm foundation on which the church could be built.

After his death and resurrection, Jesus asked the man three times if he loved him. Each time after the fisherman answered, "Yes, Lord, you know that I love you," Jesus told him to take care of his sheep.

The fisherman heard Jesus' call to ministry loud and clear, three times. He went on to become one of the foundations of the church. **That man responded to Christ's call as a witness to the story—a part of our heritage.** And his name was _Peter._

☐ Read Matthew 4:18-22; Luke 22:24-34, 54-71; John 21:15-19; Acts 2:14-41. Reflect on how Peter's understanding of God changed and how he was able to help others understand God more fully.

_____

_____

_____

_____

_____

AND THE STORY GOES ON—

Many men and women have believed. God has used them to build that bridge between God and the people. They are a part of our heritage. You remember them:

—there was _Paul,_ who told us that God speaks to all people.
—and _Barnabas_ who helped Paul start on his mission.
—and _Lydia_ who shared her gift of hospitality.
—and _Priscilla_ and _Aquila,_ both leaders in the early church.

And later:
—_Francis of Assisi,_ who made the story come alive.
—_Joan of Arc,_ who witnessed to her faith.
—and _Martin Luther,_ who told us again that we have a personal God to whom we can talk.
—and _John Wesley,_ who said that the form of religion is not enough, but we must experience God personally.
—and _Mother Teresa,_ who again taught us that God cares for each person, no matter what the person's condition.

☐ Who was a meaningful adult in your life as you grew up? Was it a Sunday school teacher? a youth leader? a parent? a friend?

Name that person. _____

This is your heritage. These are the people who have gone on before you!

AND THE STORY GOES ON—

You are a part of the time line. And you are a witness to the story, a part of the world's heritage. _You_ are the spark to ignite the future for this story. Each of us has a call to continue the story of this special relationship with God. Our call is to carry it to others in one way or another. Each of us fits into the time line, or perhaps we should call it a storyline.

☐ Read Matthew 28:19-20. Reflect on _your_ understanding of God's call to you and write your thoughts here.

_____

_____

_____

_____

_____

_____

**AND THE STORY _WILL_ GO ON,
THROUGH YOU.**

OUR FAITH STORY IN THE BIBLE

AS A TEACHER I RECOGNIZE THAT I AM A PART OF A LONG LINE OF WITNESSES

I Will Try To:

- show my faith through my relationship to my church and to my students.
- anticipate the future.
- develop an overall understanding of the needs of my students.
- work on my ability to relate to persons.
- be committed to Christ and my students.

I Will Develop and Use These Skills In:

- serious study of the Bible.
- praying for my students and my church.
- communication with students and others.
- understanding and support to students.
- matching teaching methods with student needs.
- adaptability.
- encouragement to students.

I Will Pray for My Students

Sunday	Monday	Tuesday	Wednesday	Thursday	Friday	Saturday
Thank God for my call to teach.	(list 1/5 of students)	(list 1/5 of students)	(list 1/5 of students)	(list 1/5 of students)	(list 1/5 of students)	Pray for my church and allow God to work through me as I share God's grace.

Signed _____   Date _____

From 32 WAYS TO BECOME A GREAT SUNDAY SCHOOL TEACHER
by Delia Halverson. Copyright © 1997 by Abingdon Press. Reproduced by permission.

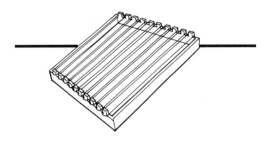

8 simplify, simplify

Purpose: To recognize what directs your life and develop ways to focus on that direction.

Oh, to be a child again! Life was so simple then! Yet, to a child life is not simple but complicated and full of decisions—decisions that must sometimes be made without the tools that experience gives us, decisions that go against the child's desires, decisions that mean complying with someone else's wishes.

No matter what our age or our circumstances in life, no matter how stripped of responsibility we structure our lives, we cannot find simplicity unless we recognize that it must truly happen on the inside before it can be faithfully expressed on the outside. Any other simplicity only wears a false mask that will fall off when we least expect it.

☐ Read Matthew 6:19-34, reflecting on how it might apply to your life.

_____

_____

_____

_____

_____

_____

☐ Paraphrase verse 21 in your own words.

_____

_____

_____

_____

_____

_____

The key is to place our spirit (or that which we hold as top priority) in God. If we concentrate on the *outward expressions* without lining our actions up with the direction that God calls us to follow (inward expressions), then we have a hollow and meaningless simplicity.

☐ Read Galatians 5:25. Our actions will indicate that which we hold important.

☐ Reread the first two chapters of Genesis, concentrating on how God is at center stage throughout the creation story.

We are indebted to God for our very existence. God gives us all that keeps us alive. God even gives us the community of people with whom we live, and the mental capacity to invent conveniences. Remember what happened after creation? We humans thought we could manage our own lives, represented by our eating forbidden fruit. We stubbornly said, "I can do it myself!"

☐ Read Philippians 4:10-13. Paraphrase the last half of verse 11 where Paul affirms that God's grace and love are greater than any of our sufferings.

_____

_____

_____

_____

☐ Reread Philippians 4:13, putting the emphasis on the words that are underlined.

_I_ can do everything through Christ who gives me
    strength.
I can do everything _through_ Christ who gives me
    strength.

How would these two readings of the verse make a difference in your decisions of what is important in life?

_____

_____

_____

_____

_____

    Go back to the creation story, and remember that we all have our times with the serpent—when we believe we can manage our lives without God. Like Adam and Eve, we must recognize our nakedness, seeing that we are nothing (or naked) without God.

☐ Look up the word _simplify_ in the dictionary. Think about the dictionary definition and the scripture passages that you just read. Now write a definition of your own that blends both the dictionary and Scripture.

_____

_____

_____

_____

_____

No matter how we try to strip away the outside clutter of our lives, unless we change our attitude toward God and look to God for our direction, we will never have simplicity inside. When we hold God's will as our central will, then our life is simplified, or laid out and easier, no matter how busy we are.

☐ Using the following definitions, write a description of your vocation.

Career: what you do for a living.
Vocation: the direction and goal of your total life, from reading the newspaper to teaching Sunday school, even to the way you respond to other drivers in traffic.

_____

_____

_____

_____

_____

_____

On Objects and Items

    In Jesus' day it was believed that being poor was a sign of God's disapproval. Perhaps this is why there was little regard for the poor. Jesus, however, taught differently. People of the early church, following Jesus' leading, spent little on themselves and had strong support for the poor.

☐ Read Matthew 19:16-24, the story of the rich young man who asked what he must do to be saved. Jesus recognized that money was the young man's god, or that which he put before anything else. What does the story say about the attitude we should have about wealth?

_____

_____

_____

_____

_____

☐ Record some of the items in your life that you could do without and still live comfortably:

_____

_____

_____

_____

☐ In order to distinguish between wants and needs, make a list of items that you feel are necessary in order for you to follow your vocation, as you have defined it here, and items that you would like to have but that are not necessary.

☐ Read Luke 12:13-21. How can this be compared to our crowded closets and bulging storerooms?

_____

_____

_____

_____

_____

☐ Take a walk through your house and decide on some things that you can give away. Is there clothing that you haven't worn in a year? Are there dishes or linens that you seldom use? Is there a small appliance that takes up storage space but you only use once a year? Can the job of that appliance be done in another way? List these items here:

_____

_____

_____

_____

_____

_____

Needs	**Wants**
_____	_____
_____	_____
_____	_____
_____	_____
_____	_____

On Worry and Frustrations

Worry and concern are two different things. Worries are fruitless, because we usually worry about things over which we have no control. Concern is an understanding of what's happening and usually leads to doing something about the situation.

☐ Read how God not only cared for the people but also taught them about taking only one day and its needs at a time. Read Exodus 16.

☐ How does hoarding the manna by the Israelites compare to our spending money for nonessentials?

_____

_____

In the Lord's Prayer, we ask God to "give us this day our daily bread." If we pray the prayer with understanding, we are asking God to give us only what we need today. We are also asking God for the ability to live one day at a time.

☐ Read Matthew 26:25-34.

☐ Pray, asking God for only what you really need today. Listen quietly to what God tells you that you truly need. Write those things down.

_____

_____

On Time and Schedules

In today's world we must be self-disciplined in order to use time well. There are many demands on our time, and most of them are good. However, God made our bodies so that we require a certain amount of rest. We do best with a balance of physical, intellectual, and spiritual time.

☐ Read Luke 2:40 and note how Jesus grew physically, intellectually, and spiritually.

☐ Use the form that follows to help you recognize just how you spend your time. Is there a good balance? How could it be adjusted?

Time Survey

Estimate your time schedule for the past week:

hours working in career _____

hours commuting or carpooling _____

hours housekeeping, shopping, and so on _____

hours as volunteer in community/church _____

hours socializing with friends _____

hours engaged in physical fitness _____

hours in recreational activities _____

hours resting and sleeping _____

hours growing closer to God through study, worship, and prayer _____

$$7 \times 24 \text{ hours} = 168$$

Now, take time to list all the activities you have taken part in during the past week. Include such items as sleeping, taking children to sports events, shopping for groceries, writing letters to relatives, commuting, and so forth.

_____

_____

_____

_____

Carefully scrutinize the activities and place the following letters beside each according to whether they are essential to:

P = physical health of yourself or your family.

E = emotional-intellectual health of yourself or your family.

S = spiritual health of yourself or your family.

Look over your list. If your time is void in one area, then you may need to search out ways to grow in that area. Review the direction that you see God calling you. That calling may require a heavier emphasis on one area, but it should not rule out the other two. Recognize that all three of these areas are important. We are told that Jesus grew in wisdom and in stature and in favor with God and people. Jesus grew in physical, emotional-intellectual, and spiritual health.[1]

On Routine Events

☐ Take four routine events (such as mowing the lawn, driving a car pool, swimming, or preparing a meal) and write down ways that you can put God at the center.

When we seek God first, then everything else falls

Example: While mowing,   discover God in the wonder of outdoors.

1. _____   _____

2. _____   _____

3. _____   _____

4. _____   _____

into proper order. Nothing should come before God's kingdom, including our desire to simplify our lives. We do not come to the Kingdom through simplicity. But when we take the Kingdom seriously, and work to better God's kingdom, then simplicity comes naturally.

What we have is a part of God's kingdom, and is a gift from God. Even our talents and intellect are gifts from God. We cannot count our achievements as fruits of our efforts, but rather as gifts from God. After all, God gave us the talents and minds to achieve. To recognize this and live for God's kingdom will make a difference in how we live.

Additional Resources

☐ Locate and review several of these resources.

Foster, Richard J. *Celebration of Discipline.* San Francisco: Harper & Row, 1988.
———. *Freedom of Simplicity.* San Francisco: Harper & Row, 1989.
Halverson, Delia. *Living Simply.* Nashville: Abingdon Press, 1996.

Do I live from the outside in
or from the inside out?
Living from outside in requires many material items to bring me joy—
Then I discover that the items have not brought the joy I expected—
So . . . I add more
—and more
—and more.
Living from the inside out brings peace
between myself and God—
Then that peace is expressed simply on the outside.

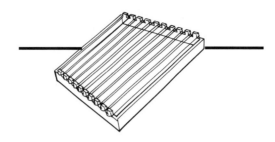

9 The Bible and Teaching Faith

Purpose: To discover our biblical heritage in sharing the faith through teaching.

Our roots run deep in Judaism, and even in the early writings of the religion, the people are commanded to pass on the faith. This was done primarily through the home, although the tribal gatherings (or extended family) played an important role by retelling the stories.

One of the ways that the faith was taught in biblical times was by reliving part of the history through tradition and ritual. The following scriptures help us to recognize the teaching potential in reliving the Passover.

☐ Read Exodus 11 and 12:1-42. Today, when Passover is observed in the Jewish home, even the children are a part of the ritual, and it becomes a learning experience. What connection do you see in these Exodus verses and our communion celebration?

_____

_____

☐ Read Mark 14:22-25; Matthew 26:26-29; and Luke 22:14-20. Note that the Gospel of John gives an account of this celebration but does not mention the bread and wine (John 13).

☐ The early church carried on this celebration, and it can be a teaching tool for us today. Read 1 Corinthians 11:23-25.

From the beginning, we were instructed by God (through Moses) to teach the faith to others, including our children.

☐ Read Deuteronomy 4:9-10; 6:1-9; and 31:12. What central theme runs through these scriptures?

_____

_____

☐ Even the psalmist instructed us to pass on the faith. Read Psalm 78:1-7.

Heritage of Teaching

You might say that the whole Bible is a story of how God taught us about the relationship for which we were created—our relationship with God. We have a great heritage of those who passed on the faith, from Abraham to the prophets, and certainly Jesus was the greatest teacher of all, not only in his words but also in his actions. As an example, look at how Jesus treated women.

☐ In Jesus' day, women were not encouraged to do

things that would distract them from household duties, such as studying or discussing theological matters. Read Luke 10:38-42. How did Jesus' statement to Martha go against that Jewish tradition?

_____

_____

☐ In Jesus' day, men did not speak to women in public. It was also unheard of for a woman who was "unclean" to touch a man. Read Mark 5:25-34 and note the response Jesus had to the "unclean" woman, a stranger, who touched him. What did he call her?

_____

_____

☐ Read Matthew 15:21-28 and Mark 7:24-30. In this case, Jesus not only spoke to a woman he did not know (and a woman of a different nationality), but he seemingly changed his attitude because of her reasoning.

☐ Read Luke 13:10-17. What Sabbath law did Jesus risk breaking for a woman?

_____

_____

☐ Jesus used women, who were excluded from education, as examples in his own teaching. Read Matthew 25:1-13; Luke 15:8-10; 18:1-8; and 13:21.

☐ The longest private conversation that Jesus had with an individual as recorded in John 4:5-41 was with a woman. What else made this a teaching situation (by example) for Jesus?

_____

_____

Affirmation of Teaching

After a lifetime of setting an example of teaching (John 13:13), Jesus included teaching in his closing statement to his disciples.

☐ Read Matthew 28:19-20. Reflect on this and paraphrase it into a commission or statement of purpose for your own teaching.

_____

_____

☐ Read the following scriptures; reflect on their statements about teaching.

Romans 12:3-8 and 1 Corinthians 12:4-6, 27–13:1

_____

_____

Ephesians 4:11-13

_____

_____

Colossians 3:15-17

_____

_____

1 Timothy 5:17

_____

_____

Called to Teach

As you've seen in these scriptures, we are each called according to our gifts. One of your specific callings is to teach. Reread your paraphrase of Matthew 28:19-20 and then spend some time quietly in prayer, asking God for guidance as you respond to that call.

☐ Now, write your response to Christ's call below. Include ways you will prepare, get to know your students, attend training sessions, share your faith, and be fully involved in the church, including worship.

_____

_____

_____

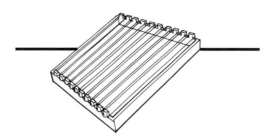

10 The Gospels

Purpose: To understand the background of Matthew, Mark, Luke, and John, and to compare stories in the various Gospels.

The word *gospel* in the New Testament comes from the Greek word *evangelion,* which means "good news." It originally meant an announcement of good news. Paul referred to the "gospel" many times, years before the first four books of the New Testament were written (Matthew, Mark, Luke, and John—which are now called the Gospels).

☐ Use a concordance to look up the word *gospel* in the New Testament and read the references. How is it used?

_____

_____

_____

_____

_____

_____

_____

_____

_____

After Jesus' death, there was expectation that he would return within a short time. During those years of waiting, the events of Jesus' life and his teachings were passed on orally. But when he did not return, and those who had known Jesus began to die, it became important to record the message in written form.

About the Gospels

In most Bibles there is introductory information before each Gospel. Read the information on Matthew, Mark, Luke, and John, and enter the information here:

☐ Which Gospel gives more of Jesus' teachings?

_____

_____

☐ Which Gospel tells more about Jesus' actions than his teachings?

_____

_____

☐ Which Gospels tell about Jesus' birth?

_____

☐ How do they tell the account differently?

_____

_____

_____

_____

_____

_____

☐ Which Gospel emphasizes Jesus' concern for people?

_____

☐ Which Gospel seems to be written primarily for a Jewish audience?

_____

☐ Summarize the background of Matthew.

_____

_____

_____

_____

_____

☐ Summarize the background of Mark.

_____

_____

_____

_____

☐ Summarize the background of Luke.

_____

_____

_____

_____

_____

☐ Summarize the background of John.

_____

_____

_____

_____

_____

_____

Compare Stories

The first three Gospels are called the Synoptic Gospels because they contain many of the same stories. The Gospel of Mark is believed to have been the first one written, and Matthew and Luke are believed to be drawn from both Mark and "Q," another version that is missing. John's version has many variances, which indicates that it was written independently.

There is a difference in the way the first Gospels handle some of the stories. Read the following scriptures and note how the story differs in the three Gospels.

☐ Matthew 9:1-8; Mark 2:1-12; Luke 5:17-26

_____

_____

_____

_____

_____

_____

Sometimes additions to a story may indicate the difference in the intended audiences.

☐ Read Matthew 15:1-20 and Mark 7:1-23. Which verses in Mark give an explanation of Jewish tradition, thereby indicating that it was written for Gentiles, who would not be familiar with these customs?

_____

_____

☐ Which verses in Matthew speak of commandments and "your tradition," thereby indicating that it was written for the Jewish believers?

_____

_____

Crucifixion and Resurrection

There are variances in the four Gospel recordings of the death and resurrection of Christ. Look at the following sections of scripture and indicate the differences on the chart on page 71. Matthew 27:32–28:8; Mark 15:21–16:8; Luke 23:26–24:9; and John 19:16–20:18.

☐ Locate the book _Gospel Parallels_ (verses of common stories and teachings printed side by side) and note differences in other stories.

_____

_____

_____

_____

_____

_____

_____

☐ In this study of the Gospels, what have you learned that you didn't realize before? Share some of your findings with a family member or another teacher.

_____

_____

Additional Resources

☐ Read or review these books.

Barclay, William. _The Daily Bible Study Bible: Matthew, Mark, Luke, John._ Louisville: Westminster/John Knox Press.

Miller, Robert J., ed. _The Complete Gospels._ Harper.

Ralph, Margaret Nutting. _Discovering the Gospels: Four Accounts of the Good News._ Mahwah, N.J.: Paulist Press, 1990.

EVENT	MATTHEW 27:32–28:8	MARK 15:21–16:8	LUKE 23:26–24:9	JOHN 19:16–20:18
Jesus carries cross				
Offer of drink				
Sign on cross				
Division of his clothing				
Words Jesus spoke				
Jesus' conversation with thieves				
Women at cross				
Darkness				
Piercing with spear				
Burial				
Easter: Women at tomb				
Stone-earthquake				
Angel				
Guards				
Disciples at tomb				
Mary Magdalene				
Whether to tell others and what to say				

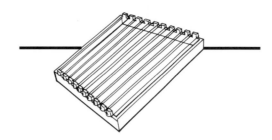

11 The Psalms

Purpose: To develop a richer understanding of the psalms.

The *Psalter* is considered the hymnal of the Bible. Indeed, the psalms were usually sung or recited, accompanied by instruments. Most of the one hundred and fifty psalms are separate and complete in themselves.

The psalms were written over a long period of time, in different circumstances, and (contrary to public opinion) by many authors. David is considered to have written only seventy-three of these chapters, and about fifty are anonymous. It was common to ascribe authorship of a piece of literature to a person well known at the time. The Hebrew translation of "a psalm of David" could as easily have read "a psalm with the style or tradition of David."

Some psalms are liturgical in nature, and others are more personal, even lamenting and crying out in anger to God. Many of them are prayers.

☐ Read the following verses and record the central theme of each.

Psalm 41:13

_____

_____

_____

_____

Psalm 72:18-19

_____

_____

_____

Psalm 89:52

_____

_____

_____

Psalm 106:48

_____

_____

_____

Psalm 150

_____

_____

_____

☐ Review the themes. Do you recognize that each is a doxology or blessing of God? These end each of the five divisions or sections in the book of Psalms.

☐ Read Psalm 137. Often the last two verses of this psalm are left out of the reading. It disturbs us to think that the Hebrews would ask God to treat infants in such a manner. However, if we recognize the context out of which the psalm comes, we can at least understand the bitterness.

☐ Consider each of the following and reflect on the psalmist's attitude, given that circumstance.

The Hebrews of that era did not believe in resurrection of the body or any afterlife. They had no concept of justice being carried out after death.

_____

_____

_____

The Babylonians had just captured them, killing many of their family members and, yes, even dashing their infants to the ground.

_____

_____

_____

Many of the psalms can be used for personal meditation. Read the following suggestions and record your reflections. As you read, recognize that the word *fear* can also be translated "awe."

☐ Read Psalm 139:1-4, 13-14 and reflect on how God is with you in everything that you do, and knows you more personally than anyone.

_____

_____

_____

_____

☐ Read the Twenty-third Psalm and then read the following paraphrase. James Taylor, the author of this paraphrase, suggests that the best way to paraphrase a familiar psalm is to take a completely different metaphor that can convey the same concepts as the original.

Mommy Holds My Hand

God is like my Mommy.
My Mommy holds my hand;
I'm not afraid.
She takes me to school in the mornings;
she lets me play in the playgrounds and the parks;
she makes me feel good.
She shows me how to cross the streets,
because she loves me.
Even when we walk among the crowds and the cars,
I am not afraid.
If I can reach her hand or her coat,
I know she's with me,
And I'm all right.
When I fall down and I'm all covered with mud
and I come home crying,
she picks me up in her arms.
She wipes my hands and dries my tears,
and I have to cry again,
because she loves me so much.
How can anything go wrong
with that kind of Mommy near me?
I want to live all my life with Mommy,
in my Mommy's home for ever and ever.[1]

☐ What other metaphors might be used to paraphrase this psalm?

_____

_____

☐ Choose one of these metaphors and create a paraphrase for the Twenty-third Psalm.

_____

_____

_____

73

you may have. Listen for the response and record your thoughts.

_____

_____

_____

☐ A psalm can be used as a prayer of confession. Read Psalm 51:1-5, 10-12, 16-17 as a prayer of confession. Write a psalm of confession for yourself.

_____

_____

_____

_____

_____

_____

☐ Read Psalm 111 and select verses that might be used as an affirmation of faith, expressing what you believe about God.

_____

_____

_____

☐ The psalmist who wrote Psalms 142 and 143 felt comfortable enough to approach God with needs and problems. Read Psalms 142:1-2 and 143:1 slowly several times. Think of a problem that you have and form it into a psalmlike prayer of your own.

_____

_____

_____

☐ Quietly pray and ask for God's help with problems

Requesting Help	Venting Frustrations	Offering Praise
Psalm 46:1	Psalm 74:1, 12	Psalm 118:1
Psalm 46:10*a*	Psalm 61:1	Psalm 98:4
Psalm 51:10	Psalm 142:1-2	Psalm 104:24

☐ We often find that a verse from the Psalms can be an instant help in time of need or an expression of praise. Read the following verses and select at least two to memorize so that you can use them spontaneously.

☐ Spend a couple of hours simply reading different psalms. Use a notebook or journal to record your thoughts as you read. Note that some psalms reflect anger, requests for strength, praise, thanksgiving, and remembering God's gifts. Here are questions you might ask yourself as you study.

- What theme does the psalm reflect?
- What makes this psalm different or unique?
- What key words or concepts do you find?
- What do the cross-references say?
- How do various translations differ?
- What does the psalm say to the author?
- What does the psalm say to you?
- How do commentaries interpret the psalm?
- How can you use the psalm in your own life?

Additional Resources

☐ Review or read several of these books.

Dunnam, Maxie. *Living the Psalms*. Nashville: Upper Room, 1990.

Kalajainen, Larry R. *Psalms for the Journey*. Nashville: Upper Room.

Keller, Phillip. *A Shepherd Looks at Psalm 23*. San Francisco: HarperCollins, 1990.

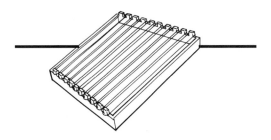

12. The Sacraments

Purpose: To grasp an understanding of the heritage of the sacraments and to deepen their meanings for us.

The word *sacrament* literally means "sacred moment." This is a time when we feel that we actually come in contact with the divine. Sacraments help us to know and experience the grace (or love) of God in Christ through taste, touch, and feeling. Most Protestant churches celebrate Baptism and Communion as sacraments, because these are the ones that Jesus took part in.

Communion

If you've been puzzled about what Communion means, don't feel alone. Much has been written about the sacrament, and to each person the meaning is unique. If it were perfectly explainable, then it would not have the impact that it does on us. Indeed, a part of the strength of the event is its mystery.

As I walked along a lake one day, I saw a radiant toddler, running toward some ducks with his mother right behind him. The mother broke small portions off a dinner roll that she had pulled from her pocket. The boy ate some of the bread and then threw a few pieces to the ducks. He then walked over to an older gentleman sitting on a bench and offered him some of the bread too. The man smiled, accepted it, and laid his hand on the boy's head.

How like our eucharist. We accept what is given to us. We receive nourishment, both physical and spiritual, and we share that with others. For celebrating Communion would never be the same if not shared with others.

When talking to young children, we refer to Communion as a time when we remember the last meal that Jesus shared with his disciples. We help them recall special meals they enjoyed with their family and friends.

☐ Recall a meal with family or friends that was joyful.

_____

_____

_____

_____

_____

_____

_____

_____

_____

_____

75

☐ Recall a farewell meal that you've had with a family member or friend. How did you feel?

_____

_____

_____

_____

Jesus was a great experiential teacher. Look at how he used the common elements of bread (the most common food of his day) and wine (the most common drink of his day, even more common than water). He used what was at hand and turned it into a real understanding of how we must make God a part of us, internally, in order to be whole—to be fulfilled, to be satisfied, to be physically and spiritually complete.

A friend of mine tells of when she was a young teenager and first recognized the significance of the symbol of taking the bread and wine (or juice) into our bodies. She was told that through the act we actually take Christ into our bodies, to be a part of us. Suddenly the thought came to her, "Well, Jesus, what does it feel like to be a girl?" Oh, that we all could feel close enough to God to speak in such a familiar way! To literally feel that Christ has become a part of us! The young shall lead us.[1]

☐ We use several names for *Communion*. Look up these words in a dictionary and write about the connecting thought between all of them.

Communion, Eucharist (Greek: thankful praise), and *Supper*

_____

_____

_____

_____

☐ Read these references in the Bible: Matthew 26:20-29; Mark 14:17-25; Luke 22:14-19; John 6:51; 1 Corinthians 11:23-26. Now read the Communion service from your church (probably found in your hymnal or book of services) and compare the scripture references to the words of the service. Are there any additional scriptures referenced in the service? Reflect on the connections that you find here.

_____

_____

_____

_____

_____

_____

_____

_____

☐ Read 1 Corinthians 11:27-29. This passage often gives us difficulty because we think that we must be perfect, or at least remember each sin and confess it, before we can receive the sacrament of Communion. In reality, this has nothing to do with our worthiness or our ability to "understand" what we are doing. Paul was referring to the gluttony of their meals. We can never be worthy by what we do, but we are worthy because God loves us. That acceptance and love we call *grace*. The grace that God gives is a "love-you-anyway" kind of love.

☐ Read Luke 15:2 and Luke 19:1-10. What was Jesus' attitude about eating with sinners?

_____

_____

_____

_____

_____

Communion

Christ became bread for us,
>> to be "eaten up" by us,
>>> completely giving of self.
We become bread for others—in our own circumstances,
>> to be "eaten up" by others,
>>> completely giving of self.
This brings the simple life for those who become one with God.
This is how they are immersed in the faith and find joy.
>> And this is how we may also find joy.[2]

Baptism

Baptism is an act of worship that should make a difference in both the person being baptized and the congregation into which he or she is baptized. There are usually vows that both take, vows of commitment to each other. Many churches observe *infant baptism* as well as *believer baptism.* In *infant baptism,* the vows are taken for the child by parents or sponsors. These vows indicate that they will raise the child in the faith. The congregational vows affirm that the members will assist in raising and nurturing the child in the faith. When the child is old enough, then he or she has the opportunity to confirm (at confirmation) the vows that were taken for him or her at baptism.

In *believer baptism,* the vows are personally made, declaring faith in Christ and an intent to follow him. Unfortunately, all too often the believer baptism or confirmation is not followed up properly by churches. Often, this is the time when questions arise and when newly baptized or confirmed persons need help in following their pledged commitment. Mentors can be particularly helpful during this time.

Persons are baptized by sprinkling, pouring, or total immersion in water. All too frequently, baptism, which makes us one in Christ, becomes a point of disagreement when we put the emphasis on the method instead of that which actually happens on the inside. It is through baptism that we receive the Holy Spirit. The method used is not as important as the actual acceptance of the Spirit.

☐ Read Matthew 3:13-17; Mark 1:9-11; Luke 3:21-22; and Acts 2:38-41; 16:11-15, 22-34.

☐ Consider how the following uses for water can bring more meaning to baptism. Add additional uses as you think of them.

Cleansing

_____

_____

_____

_____

Drinking

_____

_____

_____

Growing food

_____

_____

_____

As a power source

_____

_____

_____

Soaking the body

_____

_____

_____

77

☐ Read the baptismal vows for your church (they will probably be in the hymnal or book of services). If there are several suggested liturgies, how do they differ?

_____

_____

_____

Additional Resources

☐ For additional reading locate these books:

Stookey, Laurence Hull. *Eucharist: Christ's Feast with the Church.* Nashville: Abingdon Press, 1993.
Willimon, William. *Remember Who You Are* (on baptism). Nashville: Upper Room, 1980.
———. *Sunday Dinner* (on Communion). Nashville: Upper Room, 1981.

Baptism requires response. We cannot accept the vows of baptism without changing our lives and allowing God's power to be channeled through us.

As I watched the thundering waterfall from the bridge, I realized that a force of power flowed from the lake. Several small streams brought the water to the lake from many directions. The streams flowed quietly through the streambed, moving around rocks, rising to higher levels at times and barely trickling at other times. At the waterfall, the water, after being held in the arms of the lake, spilled over the dam in a torrent.

Is my life like this waterfall? Or is it like a child's water pistol? Both use water. Both must be filled. But one is capable of generating great power and being useful to other people. The other is capable only of generating aggravation. The waterfall is God-given power, like God showering us with love at our baptism. The water pistol must be powered by another person, and it only puts out a little squirt.

We must choose between the inexplicable power of God, filling us as we dwell in the scriptures and live day-by-day in communication with our God, or the periodic power of other people, a source refilled only according to their interests. Just as the lake is filled by several stream sources, so we are filled when we dwell in the Scriptures, study devotional materials, and surround ourselves with models and mentors. Then we lie in loving arms, as we take time to worship and live day-by-day in communication with our God. My choice of a power source comes as I look to God's direction and decide that God's choice for my life is my choice.

When we rely on the power of the waterfall, on the inexplicable power of God, we receive the capacity of transferring that power to others. We become the transformer that carries the power to others. We do this through caring acts, through sharing our understanding of God, and through praying for other people.

The choice is there. Will we constantly struggle to satisfy other people's expectations, or simply look to God for our power and direction? By choosing God, acknowledging that guidance, and receiving the waterfall of power, our lives are simplified. We move on down the river, refreshed and able to spread God's love to those along the way.[3]

I must choose the baptism I want. I must voluntarily step under the waterfall instead of waiting for someone else to squirt me with the water pistol.[4]

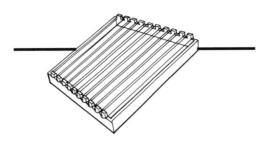

13 symbols of christianity

Purpose: To enrich your spiritual life by learning the background and reasons for symbols, and to become alert to the symbols around us.

From the very beginning, humans have used symbols to explain what we could not express in words. Christianity is no exception. The earliest known symbol that was uniquely Christian is the simple drawing of the fish. Followers of Christ in the early church were not only ostracized, but physically persecuted, often to death. In many countries it was even unlawful to be a Christian. During this time of persecution, in order to keep the faith alive, Christians worshiped in underground passages called catacombs. In public, if they wanted to know whether a person was Christian, they would casually draw on the ground a curved line using one foot. If the other person was a Christian, then he or she would draw another curved line to complete the symbol of the fish.

Today we have symbols in our churches and in our homes. Many of them relate to specific seasons, and some are used year-round.

☐ Read Mark 1:16-20 for an understanding of why they used the fish symbol. Where do we frequently use symbols of the fish today?

_____

_____

_____

Another symbol that drew importance in the days of persecution was the candle or light. Because they worshiped in catacombs or other dark, secret places, someone had to be responsible for bringing the light into the room. This was done by the acolyte. Many churches have acolytes today.

☐ Read John 1:1-9; 8:12-30. In what "dark" hour have you felt Jesus as the light to illumine your way?

_____

_____

_____

☐ Interview the person in charge of the acolytes. What do they learn during their training?

_____

_____

_____

79

☐ Talk with several acolytes. What do they enjoy about being acolytes?

_____

_____

_____

Crosses

The persecution of Christians went on until Constantine's reign as emperor of Rome. When he became a Christian in 313 C.E., Constantine put a stop to the persecution. It was not until after that time that the cross became a public symbol of Christianity. It would have been too obvious a symbol when they were being persecuted.

☐ Paul encouraged the symbolic use of the cross, even if it was not used visually. Read 1 Corinthians 1:18-25. Using a concordance, find other references to the cross in Paul's letters.

_____

_____

_____

☐ There are many different crosses used in Christianity. The most common is the Latin cross, where the lower vertical arm is longer than the others. Look at the following drawings of crosses and match them

with their symbolic significance, outlined as follows:

1. Four equal parts, which represent the four Gospels.

_____

2. Shaped as "T," traditionally the shape of the cross on which the apostle Philip died.

_____

3. Placard that was placed over Jesus' head.

_____

4. A representation of the five wounds of Christ.

_____

5. A representation of hope (read Heb. 6:19).

_____

6. A representation of the eight beatitudes.

_____

7. A representation of eternal life.

_____

8. A representation of arms stretched upward in prayer.

_____

Greek Cross	Double Cross	Forked Cross
Tau Cross	Byzantine Cross	St. Andrew's Cross
Maltese Cross	Anchor Cross	Shepherd's Cross
Jerusalem Cross	Celtic Cross	Alpha and Omega Cross

9. A representation of Christ as our shepherd.

_____

10. Uses first and last letters in the Greek alphabet, representing the inclusiveness of Christ.

_____

Letters and Monograms

Because much of the growth of the early church occurred in a Greek-speaking culture, Greek letters were used as symbols. Here are a few.

A Ω

☐ Alpha and omega, the first and last letters of the alphabet. How does this symbolize Christ?

_____

_____

T

☐ Look at the shape of the Greek letter tau. What does it remind you of that would represent Christ?

_____

_____

☐ *Ichthus* is the Greek word for fish. How does it symbolize Christ?

_____

IXθYC

_____

Chi-rho are the first two letters of the Greek word for Christ.

IHS is a popular variation of the first letters of Jesus' name.

Symbols of Sacraments

The word *sacrament* actually means "sacred moment," a time when we humans come in contact with the divine. Most Protestant churches recognize only two sacraments, Baptism and Communion, because these were acts that Jesus participated in. (For further information on sacraments, read "The Sacraments" study on page 75.)

☐ List all the different uses for water that you can think of.

_____

_____

_____

☐ Considering the many uses for water, how might water be a symbol of baptism?

_____

_____

Often the symbol of baptism is shown as three drops of water, symbolizing the Trinity.

☐ The dove (Matt. 3:13-17), shell, and rainbow are also used as symbols of baptism. How can these symbols be interpreted?

_____

_____

_____

☐ Bread or wheat and grapes or the chalice are symbols of Communion or the Last Supper. Read the following scripture passages and reflect on their connection to our Communion.

Luke 22:15-20

_____

_____

_____

1 Corinthians 11:23-26

_____

81

Colors and Symbols of the Christian Year

 *Advent* begins four Sundays before Christmas. It is a time when we get ready to celebrate Christ's coming. The color for Advent may be purple, violet, or blue. A symbol for Advent is the candle. This helps us to remember that Christ brought light into our lives. We use four candles to represent the four weeks of Advent. Four can also represent the four Gospels.

 *Christmas Season* begins on Christmas Day and continues for twelve days. We celebrate Christ's birthday, remembering that he was our greatest gift. The color for Christmas is white. A symbol for Christmas is the manger.

☐ Besides purple or blue for royalty, the colors used in Advent and Christmas are green (living forever), red (Christ's blood), and gold (also royalty). What other symbols for Advent and Christmas do you know, and what do they represent?

_____

_____

_____

_____

 *Epiphany Season* is the period beginning January 6—from Epiphany to Ash Wednesday, the beginning of Lent. It is a time when we remember the visit of the wise men and that Christ came for *all* the world. Often we learn about missions during this time. The color for Epiphany is green. Although we do not know whether the wise men were actually kings, nor do we know how many wise men there really were, we sometimes use three crowns as a symbol for Epiphany.

☐ During Epiphany we also recognize how Jesus grew in a normal Hebrew family. Read Matthew 2:1-18 and Luke 2:41-51.

Lent begins on Ash Wednesday and ends with Palm Sunday. The Lenten season lasts forty days (not counting Sundays). Lent is a time when we think about how we can be better people and live the kind of life that Jesus asked us to live. It is a good time to remember the teachings of Jesus. The color for Lent may be violet or purple. On Good Friday we use black. We call Good Friday (the day that Jesus was killed) "good" because we know what happened afterward. We know that Jesus loved us so much he would do anything for us, even die. Symbols for Lent are the cross and the crown of thorns that was placed on his head.

☐ Take a few minutes to think about the circumstances of the last week of Jesus' life. Many of those events give us other symbols for Lent. The cross is usually draped with black on Good Friday. What are some of the other symbols for Lent and Holy Week, and what might they mean? Reread the narrative of the final week for ideas (Matt. 21–27; Mark 11–15; Luke 19:28–23:56; John 12:12–19:42).

_____

_____

_____

_____

 *Easter Season* begins with Easter and includes six other Sundays before Pentecost. It is the most important time in the Christian year because we remember that God would not let Jesus stay dead—God brought Jesus back to life. We know that in a special way Jesus can be with us always. The color for Easter is white. A symbol for Easter is the butterfly, because the butterfly seems dead and then bursts forth with life.

☐ Anything that creates life from something apparently dead (bulbs, seeds, eggs) and anything symbolizing new life are often used as symbols for Easter. What other symbols do you know that represent Easter, and what do they mean? You may want to read Matthew 28:1-10; Mark 16:1-8; Luke 24:1-12; John 20:1-18 for ideas.

_____

_____

_____

_____

Pentecost is the fiftieth day after Easter. Pentecost was a Jewish celebration when Jesus' friends were together after his death. This is the time that the Holy Spirit came, and they knew that God was a part of them. Symbols for Pentecost are the dove and flame, and the color is red.

☐ Read Acts 2:1-13 for the account of Pentecost.

Between Pentecost and the next Advent is what we often call the Season After Pentecost; some churches call it Kingdomtide. The color is green, and it is a time for growth in our faith. Growth is often symbolized with a green sprout.[1]

Windows and Pictures

Until relatively recent times, learning to read was available only to a privileged few. Stained-glass windows and pictures were the symbols of stories in the Bible. These acted as reminders of the stories and truths. Symbols were often incorporated into the stained glass and the paintings.

☐ Find out about the history of any stained-glass win-

dows or pictures that are in your church building.

_____

_____

_____

Look for Symbols

Spend some time in your church building, particularly in the worship area, and look for ways that symbols are used. Look at the outside architecture too. Four-panel doors often incorporate the cross into the design. In fact, these became popular in homes because of their representation of the cross. Anything with three corners or three identical units represents the Trinity, and anything with four parts can represent the four Gospels. The arches represent reaching up to heaven, and the raised area in front of the sanctuary represents the importance of Christ and the Word. Circles represent God's unending love.

☐ What other symbols do you find, and what do they represent?

_____

_____

_____

There are a number of books that offer information about the many symbols used throughout Christendom. A check with your church or public library will reveal several good sources, or talk with persons on the worship committee or altar guild.

Additional Resources

☐ Review any of these books:

Moe, Dean. *Christian Symbols Handbook.* Minneapolis: Augsburg Fortress, 1985.
Whittemore, Carroll E. *Symbols of the Church.* Nashville: Abingdon Press, rev. ed. 1987.

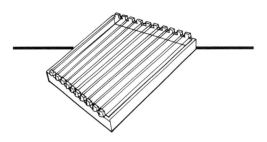

14 worship

Purpose: To enrich your spirituality through a better understanding of worship.

There is a story of a young boy who stood in his father's study door, and simply kept standing. His father finally looked up at him and asked, "Can I do something for you?" The boy answered, "Nope. I'm just lookin' and lovin'."

This is the kind of adoration that we offer God in worship. We do not love God because of some circumstance, we simply look and love. However, worship is more than that. Worship offers us the opportunity to come into a personal relationship with God, and our corporate worship services give us the opportunity to search this relationship in the company of others.

☐ Recall a time that you have seen a child express awe over something, seemingly in worship. (This can be any time, any place. Consider such times as seeing a sprout come from an apparently dead bulb, exhilaration over an animal, or unguarded joy over some new understanding.)

_____

_____

_____

_____

☐ Read Mark 10:13-16. How does this action of Jesus relate to our attitude toward worship of God?

_____

_____

_____

_____

_____

☐ Reflect on this statement and make notes on your reflection: *If we understood all there is to know about God, then God would not be God.*

_____

_____

_____

_____

☐ Read Exodus 3:1-14. Recall an "ah-ha" time that you had with God, a time when you had a glimpse of God that was a revelation. This might be called a "bush burning" experience with God.

_____

_____

_____

_____

_____

_____

_____

☐ Using a concordance, look up words such as *worship, praise, devotion, pray,* and *reverence.* Read some of the passages. Which ones speak of the way we worship?

_____

_____

_____

_____

_____

_____

_____

Order of Worship

There is a basic pattern for worship that most congregations use. This pattern has four parts: *entrance or*

gathering, proclamation and response, thanksgiving and communion, and *sending forth.*

☐ Look at a worship bulletin from your church or think about your worship service and identify the parts of the service that fall into the four categories.

_____

_____

_____

☐ Go through the bulletin again and mark the times we talk to God and times God talks to us. (Sometimes that "talking" is done through a worship leader or the choir. Some parts of the service may do one or the other on a given Sunday.)

We talk to God.	God talks to us.

☐ Compare the "Guide for Understanding the Order of Worship" on page 86 with your own worship bulletin. What parts are in your service (they may be titled differently)? If your church has different parts, write down simple descriptive sentences about them.

_____

_____

_____

A Guide for understanding the Order of Worship

Prelude　　　　　　　　We prepare for worship as we listen quietly to music.

Concerns of the Church　　We hear of how we care for our church family, and we record our presence, looking at the names of those around us.

Meditation and Silent Confession　　We think of things about our life we would like to change and ask God to help us.

Call to Worship　　　　We prepare for worship by reading with the pastor.

First Hymn　　　　　　We praise God with song.

Prayer of Invocation　　This is our opening prayer, asking God to be with us.

Our Lord's Prayer　　　We pray together a prayer that Jesus taught us.

Gloria Patri　　　　　We sing a very old song of praise to God.

Children's Message　　The pastor conducts a special time for children.

Morning Prayers　　　In our prayers, we especially remember persons in need, and joys that we have received.

Doxology　　　　　　We sing praise to God in response to the gifts given us.

Offertory　　　　　　We enjoy music as we give back to God some of what is given us.

Ministry of Music　　Sometimes the choir sings, and sometimes we have other music. The music praises God, and sometimes God talks to us through music.

Scripture　　　　　　We hear God's word from the Bible.

Message　　　　　　We hear the pastor explain God's Word. What is God (through the pastor) asking you to do?

Closing Hymn　　　　We dedicate (promise) to do God's work.

Benediction　　　　　The pastor sends us out in the world to care.

Congregational Response　　We sing that God's love is through all the world, and we will take it to others.

Postlude　　　　　　Music plays, sending us out to take God to others.[1]

From 32 WAYS TO BECOME A GREAT SUNDAY SCHOOL TEACHER
by Delia Halverson. Copyright © 1997 by Abingdon Press. Reproduced by permission.

Sacraments

The word *sacrament* means, literally, "sacred moments." These are special times when we encounter God in a very personal way. If you have not read our study "The Sacraments," look at page 75 for a brief definition of them.

☐ Reflect on the last times you took part in the sacraments. What could you have done to feel closer to God during those times?

Baptism:

_____

_____

_____

_____

Communion:

_____

_____

_____

_____

☐ What physical worship aids in your sanctuary help to lift your spirit and connect you to God? These may be symbols, banners, colors, etc. (Our study "Symbols of Christianity" on page 79 will give you more insight here.)

_____

_____

_____

_____

☐ What might you suggest to your worship committee (objects or actions) that would enhance the worship for you? Consider writing a letter with your suggestions.

_____

_____

_____

_____

_____

☐ After completing this study area, take part in another worship service at your church and write how the study has enhanced your worship. How did you feel more attuned with God during the service?

_____

_____

_____

_____

Additional Resources

☐ For additional reading locate the following books:

Hickman, Hoyt L. *United Methodist Altars.* Nashville: Abingdon Press, 1984.

———. *A Primer for Church Worship.* Nashville: Abingdon Press, 1984.

Westerhoff III, John, and William Willimon. *Liturgy and Learning Through the Life Cycle.* Akron, Ohio: OSL Publications, 1994.

White, James F. *A Brief History of Christian Worship.* Nashville: Abingdon Press, 1993.

———. *Introduction to Christian Worship,* rev. ed. Nashville: Abingdon Press, 1990.

Willimon, William. *Word, Water, Wine, and Bread.* Valley Forge, Pa.: Judson Press, 1980.

THE WEFT: PRACTICAL APPLICATION

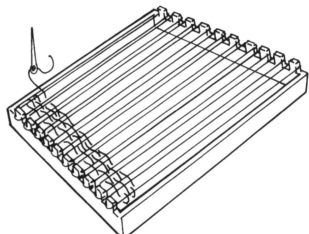

15 Death, Illness, and Other Crises

Purpose: To help you deal with crises that may affect your students. By considering it before it happens, we are better able to recognize and assist a student during crisis.

When we have only an hour (and sometimes less) a week to be with our students, we often ignore crises in their lives. Sometimes it is because we are not even aware of them. We may ignore the symptoms, not recognizing them as signals and dismissing them as unimportant or as a "stage."

These crises affect learning ability, attention span, and the relationship the student has with others. Our physical, emotional, and spiritual development all interact. Therefore, it is important not only to be aware of a crisis in a student's life but to help the student grow through it spiritually.

☐ Look up the word *crisis in* the dictionary.

_____

_____

_____

☐ Make a list of possible crises that might happen (or have happened) to students in your class. (Include physical, emotional, financial, and spiritual crises.)

_____

_____

_____

☐ Recall a bereavement, illness, divorce, or other crisis a class member suffered, of which you were unaware until its climax.

_____

_____

_____

_____

Feelings

Feelings are bodily signals that indicate an emotional state. Feelings are neither good nor bad. Feelings just *are*.

☐ What is the first crisis that you remember as a child?

_____

_____

_____

_____

_____

☐ Recall your *feelings* at that time.

_____

_____

_____

_____

☐ List some crises that children may have, but which we adults would consider smaller worries. (Include changing schools, parent dating, death of pet, older sibling leaving home.) How might the child feel?

_____

_____

_____

_____

_____

_____

_____

_____

We cannot choose whether or not to have certain feelings, but we *can* choose what we do with them and how we express them. If a student expresses anger through destructive or hurting behavior, whether physical or emotional, offer suggestions for substitute behaviors that can be used to release the anger. Help the student to recognize the consequences of such action. Work toward affirmative actions.

With children, you may ask, "Can you stop this behavior, or do you need some help in stopping?" Assure the child that it's O.K. if he or she needs help in stopping. That's what you are there for.

With any age, help the student to recognize that you love and approve of the student, even while disapproving of the behavior. Sometimes persons may not even realize just why they are acting in an inappropriate manner. If so, give them an educated guess as to why. If they agree with your guess or remain neutral, then this is probably the reason. If they disagree, they will probably then come to recognize the reason.

Stages of Grief

Most often we think of grief only in connection with death. In reality, any loss (death, job, relationship) creates an atmosphere for grief. It helps to recognize stages of grief and the reactions we encounter.

Stage 1—*Early Responses*

A time of shock and numbness. Often denial that it has happened. This helps to get us through the immediate details necessary after a death or other loss.

If a period of extreme illness precedes death, adults sometimes process this stage before death. Young children, however, seldom grasp the seriousness of the illness and the finality of death, and so may not process this stage prior to the death.

Stage 2—*Acute Grief*

This stage includes sadness and depression. The person often feels anger, anxiety, and fear. Guilt is not uncommon, particularly with children. They may believe that they could have done something, acted differently, or left some wish unsaid in order to prevent the loss.

This stage is characterized by restless sleep, loss of appetite, weight loss, and disorganization or withdrawal. Children may regress into patterns they have outgrown, such as bed-wetting, thumb-sucking, and so forth.

Stage 3—*Rebuilding or Adjustment*

Finally we begin the slow process of acceptance and adjustment. Too often, at a time when we need support from friends, those around us return to "life as normal." After a death, remembering happy times with the person is important during this stage of adjustment.

Children need help as they reorganize their lives and establish their directions. Since the significant adults around them usually find that they need to move in new directions, this often conflicts with the child's desire to return their lives to old established patterns.

☐ Recall persons you have known who have gone through these stages. Note the actions that demonstrated the stages.

Early Responses

_____

_____

_____

_____

_____

_____

Acute Grief

_____

_____

_____

_____

_____

_____

_____

_____

Rebuilding or Adjustment

_____

_____

_____

_____

_____

_____

Children and adults move back and forth through these stages as they work with their grief. Because children cannot verbally express their feelings well, they will often become withdrawn or rebellious. Life has changed, but they feel powerless to do anything about it.

Age Concepts of Death and Loss, and Symptoms of Grieving

Ages 0-3 Years

The perception of death at this age is not well defined. These children find separation of any type often as threatening as death.

Ages 3-5 Years

These children seldom accept death or any other loss as final. Since their concept of time is not developed, they often speak of the person as returning or as if there were a marriage being reconciled. They will have feelings about the loss that they have difficulty expressing because of their lack of abstract thinking and limited language skills. Sometimes, however, they are open in sharing feelings with others, even strangers. They will check reactions to find support and to learn how they are expected to feel.

Often children don't recognize that others may be caught up in their own grief, and that this is the reason they are ignored. They may believe this action is evidence of the loss being their fault. Imagined responsibility for the loss is typical.

Behavior changes are typical in children's eating and sleeping, and bowel and bladder functions. They may also exhibit excessive clinging, tantrums, thumb-sucking, and so on. This is true of all children under stress. Their loss of security is intensified through fears of the dark, new places, being left alone, being taken away, and a parent's death.

You can expect emotional swings. The child may be crying one moment and engrossed in happy play the next.

Ages 5-9 Years

Children in this age range typically see death or loss as a punishment and often imagine that the loss is brought on in secret by some outside, invisible force. They may also feel that their thinking has in some secret way caused the loss. Because they operate in a right-wrong understanding of the world, they often believe that life will be happy if one is good, and life will have loss and problems will occur if one is bad.

These children experience confusion, with denial and acceptance, and cannot comprehend that death or someone else's problems will happen to or affect them.

Age 9 Years and Above

Children of this age are better able to grasp cause and effect regarding life events. Their abstract thinking is developing and they can reason better.

At this age children begin to recognize that there is an end to the physical life as we know it. They can begin to grasp the fact that death is biologically caused and see death as irreversible. Although they still wrestle with the "fairness" of death and other losses, these crises are now better understood as something that happens to everyone and as a part of life.

Untimely Deaths or Losses

"Why me?" is the typical response to untimely deaths or losses. This partially stems from an attitude that God purposely causes bad things to happen. Although we cannot explain why bad things happen to good people and to young people, we can help our students appreciate the goodness of God and recognize the fact that God does not "zap" us dead or send losses to teach us a lesson. They can better appreciate the grieving God who suffers *with* us.

We were made by God in God's own image, with an ability to choose. We call this gift our free will. Without free will we would only be puppets or robots. Deaths or other losses that seem unfair may happen when we make wrong choices, or sometimes our society has made a wrong choice in the past. Or perhaps we are still learning about God's scientific laws.

☐ Read Genesis 1:26-31. Reflect on how being created in God's image includes being given a free will to choose positive or negative actions.

_____

_____

_____

_____

_____

☐ God respects our free choice. Leslie Weatherhead explains God's will in his book *The Will of God,* as summarized here:

1. In the *intentional or original will,* God pours out goodness such as a parent longs to do for the child. God sets a plan for us, and a part of that plan is our free will. We can choose our own actions, whether they be wise or not.
2. As we go about our lives we choose. Those choices and other circumstances in the world establish the *circumstantial will* of God. In those circumstances, and because God chooses to let us experience the consequences of our choices, God's will is happening. We are not promised that things will be easy, only that God will help us through life.
3. The *ultimate will* of God comes about when we turn the circumstances over to God and allow God to work through us in all circumstances. We become even clos-

er to God, and the ultimate will is greater than the original or intentional will.

☐ Consider the death of a child caused by a drunk driver. How might you talk with those questioning it by using Weatherhead's three wills of God?

_____

_____

_____

_____

_____

_____

Suggestions for Helping Children and Adults Deal with Death

☐ Discuss death naturally before it occurs. Death is a time when the *you* (the part that laughs when you are happy and that cries when you are sad) leaves the body. We sometimes call this part of us our soul.

☐ Use seeds, flower bulbs, cemeteries, newspaper reports, and so on as conversational springboards. Recognize God's plan for cycles.

☐ Share the sorrow, even with children. If a pet dies and a child asks questions of whether the pet will go to heaven, say you don't know but you know that God has a plan. It's O.K. to be unsure, because we trust God.

☐ Stress a child's own security and your continuing love and concern for the child or adult. "We don't turn off love when someone dies."

☐ Be alert to *missing* times. Say, "We miss ____, don't we?" Share happy memories. Help children write stories of good times shared with the person who died.

☐ Include children in grief. Cry openly, but not hysterically. Give extra security.

☐ Continue routines and rituals. Physical activities release strain. Your class may be the only stability the child finds in an unstable world.

☐ Give simple, physical reasons for death, *not* that the person was "taken by God."

☐ We call God's plan for after death "heaven" although we don't know just what it's like. Before birth we didn't know what life would be like, but we're glad we were born.

☐ Encourage questions. Express your belief, but don't hesitate to acknowledge a question you are still wrestling with. Work on it together.

☐ With children, the question "Why do people die?" may mean, "Are you going to die and leave me?" Tell them that usually people live to be very old before they die. We don't expect to die for a long time. Recognize others who love and care for the child too.

☐ Read additional suggestions for children and youth about death and heaven in *How Do Our Children Grow?* (Delia Halverson, Abingdon Press, 1993).

Affirmative Action for a Crisis

A caring attitude for the student in crisis, one that doesn't smother, is the most affirmative action a class can take. We should not ignore or deny the hurts and the loss that a student feels, but encourage the person to become a part of doing something for others. This might be a mission project, particularly one that requires physical energy. Physical activity helps with the healing.

Children may need help in building self-control. You might try some games such as "Captain, May I" or "Statue." Or experiment with leaning in one direction as far as possible without losing your balance.

You may never be approached by a student concerning a crisis, although you may be aware of it. Our society sends out the signal that we should be strong and deal with our problems alone.

Let the person know that he or she has "permission" to talk personally to you about the crisis at any time. If it is a child, you might take him or her aside and say, "You may ask me any questions you want now, and you can come to me any time with questions."

You need not rush into conversations, but use active listening, feeding back to the person some comments or questions that encourage more than yes and no answers. You can pick up on hidden thoughts by saying, "I hear you saying . . ." It also helps if you can share similar situations from your life, not to give answers to the problem but to help the person work through the particulars.

☐ Consider some similar situations from your life that you might share with a person dealing with these crises:

Death

_____

_____

_____

_____

Loss of relationship

_____

_____

_____

_____

Illness

_____

_____

_____

_____

_____

Change in location/
job/circumstances

_____

_____

_____

_____

_____

Whether the student shares openly with you or not, you can help the student to recognize that God is always with us to help us. Sometimes we can appreciate that closeness by thinking of God as being like the air we breathe. We cannot see the air, but we can feel it and we can see the results of the air. It also brings us life. (For information on a "Breath Prayer" see page 54.)

Additional Resources

☐ Review and read the following books:

Carter, Velma, and Lynn Leavenworth. *Caught in the Middle: Children of Divorce.* Valley Forge, Pa.: Judson Press, 1985.

Coleman, Wendy. *Attention Deficit Disorders, Hyperactivity & Associated Disorders.* Madison, Wis.: Calliope Books, 1993.

Ervin, Nancy. *Kids on the Move.* Birmingham: Conquest Corp., 1989.

Halverson, Delia. *How Do Our Children Grow?* Nashville: Abingdon Press, 1993 (chap. on helping children and youth understand death).

Jewett, Claudia. *Helping Children Cope with Separation and Loss.* Boston: Harvard Common Press, 1982.

Lester, Andrew, ed. *When Children Suffer: A Sourcebook for Ministry with Children in Crisis.* Philadelphia: Westminster Press, 1987.

Weatherhead, Leslie D. *The Will of God.* Nashville/New York: Abingdon Press, 1972.

DEATH, ILLNESS, AND OTHER CRISES

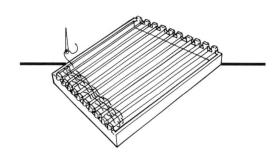

16 Incorporating Stewardship and Mission

Purpose: To develop ways to incorporate learning opportunities for stewardship and mission into any lesson.

Stewardship has become an avoided word around churches. Perhaps that is because we most often associate it with asking people to give money. Consequently, teachers usually ignore stewardship unless it's printed in the curriculum.

In reality, the word *steward* is defined as one who manages the affairs of another. With that understanding, as stewards we manage the affairs of God, whether that be the earth's resources, our time, our abilities, our material possessions, or yes, even our money.

Stewardship, however, cannot happen effectively without its accompanying mission. One is not complete without the other. If we are true stewards of our gifts from God, then we will use them for others.

☐ Read the twenty-fifth chapter of Matthew.

☐ What did Jesus say in these stories about our responsibility as stewards and our mission (or call) to care for God's people?

_____

_____

_____

_____

_____

_____

_____

☐ Paraphrase or give one-sentence summaries for these scriptures that help us recognize our responsibility in stewardship and mission.

Examples:
Psalm 133:1 *(How good it is for us all to live happily together.)*
Matthew 25:31-46 *(Jesus told a story about how, when we care for other people, it's like caring for Jesus.)*

Proverbs 17:17*a*

_____

_____

_____

Isaiah 35:3

_____

_____

Matthew 5:44

_____

_____

Matthew 22:37-40

_____

_____

Luke 19:1-10

_____

_____

John 6:1-15

_____

_____

John 13:1-20

_____

_____

_____

John 15:12

_____

_____

_____

1 Corinthians 13

_____

_____

_____

Ephesians 4:1-6

_____

_____

_____

Philippians 2:13

_____

_____

_____

Hebrews 13:20-21

_____

_____

_____

1 John 4:7-8

_____

_____

_____

Goals and Ages

No matter what the age, one important factor in encouraging stewardship and mission is to affirm each student in his or her own uniqueness and encourage and applaud any acts of caring. Spend some time helping students discover their own special gifts, and help them recognize that those talents are truly a gift *from* God, to be used in turn *for* God.

Very young children can:
- build appreciation of themselves, as a foundation for understanding how to care for others.
- enjoy a trusting environment as a foundation of future understanding.
- grow, nourished with praise for their positive actions.
- enjoy parallel play as they build social skills.
- use play items from different races and cultures.

Children ages 3 to 6 can:
- enjoy songs, stories, and games from different cultures (experience now, label later).
- learn an occasional word for names and numbers in other languages.
- know persons of different cultures who have positive attitudes.
- develop group skills that lead to a sense of belonging and love for others.
- grow in pride in the church family and recognize ways the church helps others.
- recognize that we come together to worship and study and then go out to serve.
- appreciate their own talents and abilities.
- find simple ways to use their abilities to help others.

Children in grades 1 to 3 can:
- accept responsibility for their own actions and how their actions affect others.
- as their geography knowledge grows, recognize how Christians around the world tell and show others what God has done.
- expand experiences with songs, games, stories, etc.
- recognize that people worship differently.
- meet more people from different cultures.
- see situations from different viewpoints.
- manage their time (be good stewards of time).
- learn that money is of God's creation and belongs to God.
- recognize that money is a result of the ways we use our talents.
- see different ways money functions in church.

- expand understanding of service to others outside the church and devise ways the class can act in mission.

Children in grades 4 to 6 can:
- understand justice as everyone's right to basic needs and how justice differs from fairness.
- distinguish between independence and interdependence.
- develop talents to use as stewards.
- see themselves through another's eyes.
- "stand in the moccasins of others."
- relate facts of the world to others' lives.
- research and converse to find their own answers about other cultures.
- appreciate God's concern for *all*.
- become aware of ways to be in mission in everyday life and on special projects.[1]

Youth and adults can:
- work with the statements for grades 4 to 6.
- undertake extensive projects to use their gifts for others.
- involve others in understanding stewardship and mission.
- assume church leadership in these areas.

Ways We Signal Bias

Some actions that unconsciously signal bias are so much a part of our culture that we have difficulty recognizing them. These cause persons to believe that they are inadequate because of their culture, age, sex, race, or ability. If you alert yourself to these circumstances you can begin to correct them. They might include:

- references to Native Americans as Indians or savages.
- persons from other cultures pictured *only* in native costumes.
- books, toys, posters, etc. of the dominate culture only.
- men and women pictured in stereotypical roles or careers
- calling on boys more than girls.
- lack of pictures showing persons with handicapping conditions doing ordinary activities.
- showing older persons in inactive situations only.
- references to minorities in demeaning roles.
- using black and white for good and bad.

☐ Check your curriculum, books, songs, and teaching pictures for signals of any of these biases. What did you find?

_____

_____

_____

_____

☐ How can you be racially and culturally inclusive?

_____

_____

_____

_____

☐ How can you be sexually inclusive?

_____

_____

_____

_____

☐ How can you help students to appreciate different ages?

_____

_____

_____

☐ How can you help students understand and appreciate persons with handicapping conditions?

_____

_____

_____

_____

Differences and Multicultural Appreciation

One way to enable students to care for other people is to help them celebrate the differentness that we all have. A positive approach in assisting students in recognizing their differences helps to overcome biased attitudes. Here are two examples of ways that you can accomplish this in the classroom.

1. Ask each student to name a favorite movie, book, toy, or vacation and then talk about how we all have different likes and dislikes. Ask what the world would be like if we were all alike.
2. Create disabling circumstances for students by using experiences such as trust walks (a student is blindfolded and led around by another student), wheelchairs, earplugs.

For more ideas, see page 27 of *Helping Children Care for God's People* (Abingdon Press, 1994).

Justice

"Justice" and "equality" are not always the same. Jesus taught the difference in one of his parables.

☐ Read Matthew 20:1-16. How was the action in the story just but not equal?

_____

_____

_____

☐ Everyone has the right to have common needs filled. List below the needs that we all have in these categories.

Physical needs

_____

_____

_____

Emotional needs

_____

_____

_____

Intellectual needs

_____

_____

_____

Spiritual needs

_____

_____

_____

Classroom Atmosphere

We can talk about stewardship and mission until we are blue in the face and still have little impact if we don't help our students experience it. Give students an opportunity in the classroom to fulfill the membership vows of your church. The vows probably include prayers (arrange for a time or place to note prayer requests), presence (register attendance), gifts (opportunity for offering, knowing what it is used for), and service (opportunity to record or recognize acts of kindness during each week).

Create a stewardship environment in the classroom.

Help the students to take pride in caring for God's world and sharing with others. Talk up the caring opportunities that your church offers and ways the church itself exhibits stewardship.

☐ Gather materials about the mission or caring opportunities that your church supports. List them below. You may have to do some research here, because we are not always aware of all of them, particularly those that are supported by money that is sent to a denominational office.

_____

_____

_____

_____

☐ Prayerfully consider the following and check changes you will make in your classroom in order to convey the message of stewardship and mission:

____Recycle paper and curriculum.
____Avoid Styrofoam.
____Recycle items with pride.
____Avoid using food items unless they will be eaten.
____Use inclusive language wherever possible.
____Lift up examples of persons known to students.
____Plan projects that care for others.
____Ask students to share ways they've been of service to others.
____Avoid stereotyping cultures, ethnic backgrounds, etc.
____When learning about other cultures, distinguish between the traditional dress, customs, and houses, and those most often used today.
____Use pictures featuring persons of different races, not just "token" persons.
____Find pictures that show family life in different social environments.
____Use pictures including persons with physical impairments in everyday situations, but not calling attention to the impairment.
____Review all books in the classroom and discard those that do not live up to the criteria listed in the chart that follows.
____Create a file of pictures that show people with differences working and playing together.
____Use pictures that offer a balance of men and

women doing jobs in and outside the home.

_____Show pictures that illustrate a balance of men and women doing various kinds of work (mechanic, doctor, salesperson, teacher, beautician, et al.).

_____Encourage both male and female participation in *all* activities.

_____Add any additional changes.

_____

_____

_____

_____

Experiencing

We each have the gifts that God gave us. One of your gifts is an ability to teach. The church gives you the opportunity to use your gift. You do this by helping students recognize their own gifts and by creating opportunities for them to share the gospel and care for others.

The following list will give you contacts for various agencies and projects.

Project Possibilities

Family work camp—Several churches have sponsored family work camps to do some construction work and some Vacation Bible School leadership. Look through the organizations listed below for some possibilities. These churches have had family work camp experiences:

St. Paul's UMC	First UMC
5501 Main,	116 NE Perry Ave.,
Houston, TX	Peoria, IL
77004	61603-3687
(713)528-0527	(309)673-3641

Grow a garden—There are several options here. You may want to raise food that can be shared with a food kitchen or families who are in need. Growing a multicultural garden not only gives an experience of mission, but also introduces students to food of other cultures.

Supply a meal—This may be done through a local mission or by locating a family that needs it and inviting them to come in and share a meal. You can also be in mission by taking a meal to persons who are coming home from the hospital and unable to fix a meal themselves.

Another idea is to make lunchbox meals for adults working in such projects as Habitat for Humanity.

Bake for others—Many homeless shelters would enjoy home-baked bread or cookies. This is an activity that all ages can do, stirring and kneading together.

Share song/friendship pet—Arrange with

Evaluate Children's Books

Evaluate the characters
- What characters are authentic in their actions?
- What characters only reflect stereotype personalities?
- Look at the language. Is it accurate in the character's situation, or is it stereotyped?
- Are their lifestyles current, or do they reflect lifestyles that we equated with that particular culture in past years?
- Are strengths and weaknesses reflective of persons everywhere or is there an undercurrent stereotype message?
- Do the characters change and come to new insights with the story?

Evaluate the situation
- Is there a positive emphasis on those attributes that everyone has?
- Are the characters given independence in their actions, or are they treated like puppets, with no choices?
- Are the characters allowed to suffer the consequences of their actions as well as solve problems and reap any rewards?

Evaluate illustrations
- Are the illustrations respectful of ethnic, age, cultural, economic, ability, and sexual differences and commonality?
- Do the illustrations help to convey the message of the text, or do they place prominence on portions of the story that are minor?
- Is the art style appropriate to the story and the characters, or does it give hidden messages of bias?

(Adapted from Bonnie Neugebauer in Stacey York, *Roots and Wings* [St. Paul, Minn.: Redleaf Press, 1991], p. 57)

INCORPORATING STEWARDSHIP AND MISSION

local nursing homes or retirement facilities to visit. You might also arrange to deliver an audiotape of the church service to a specific shut-in each week and get to know the person well. These people enjoy having your pets visit with you, but be sure to check for approval. St. Marks UMC in Lincoln, Nebraska, has a program called PAWS (Pets Are Working Saints) where pets visit in local nursing homes.

Visit mission sites—Find out locations of church mission sites near your community and arrange to visit.

Adopt a room/garden space—Arrange to adopt a church classroom or part of the landscaping around the church and apply fresh paint or keep it weeded and watered.

Plant a tree—Arrange to plant a tree in a park or along a roadway to refurbish the earth. Or raise money for trees to be replanted in the rain forests that have been destroyed.

Pray for missionaries and their children—Send for calendars that list the birthdays of missionary children (also one for the adults). Pray for those who are listed each day, and even write to them on their birthday. (GBOBM Service Center, 7820 Reading Rd., Caller No. 1800, Cincinnati, OH 45222-1800)

Plan a Souper Bowl—Arrange to collect money for a local soup kitchen on Super Bowl Sunday, using a soup kettle to collect. Call Spring Valley Presbyterian Church, 125 Sparkleberry Ln., Columbia, SC 29223 (1-800) 358-SOUP.

Organizations

Appalachia Service Project—4523 Bristol Hwy., Piney Flats, TN 37686-5201. This is a repair/home building ministry for economically disadvantaged people, using a Christian perspective. Provides materials for study ahead of time.

One week during the summer and a weekend in the spring are set aside specifically for families (ages six years and up). Other weekends may be arranged. First UMC at Peoria, Illinois, have gone as families several times.

Baptist Peace Fellowship—499 Patterson St., Memphis, TN 38111.

Bethesda Learning Center Work Camp—P.O. Box 538, Bethesda, OH 43719-0538. (614) 484-4705. They have several work camps for youth and adults, and are considering the possibility of families.

Coordination for Parish Projects—Lutheran World Relief, 390 Park Ave. S., New York, NY 10016.

Children's Fund for Christian Mission—P.O. Box 840, Nashville, TN 37202. Find out about the mission and contribute to this fund.

CROP—An ecumenical organization that provides food, seeds, tools, and various other kinds of appropriate technology to those without—Church World Service, P.O. Box 968, Elkhart, IN 46515. They provide hunger educational materials and design a CROP Walk every year to raise money for hunger.

ECHO (Educational Concerns for Hunger Organization)—17430 Durrance Rd., North Ft. Myers, FL 33917-2200. 1-941-543-3246. Uses volunteer help to research, develop, and distribute seeds and information on trees, edible plants, and small animals to deprived countries. Also provides intern training and networking newsletter for missionaries and other nonprofit workers in Third World countries. Also has VBS program and has materials on edible landscaping. You may secure seeds for experimenting in your own garden.

Friends of the Americas—An organization through which you may send a Christmas box to children and families who live in depived areas of Latin America. For information on the Christmas Box Project, contact Friends of the Americas, 1024 North Foster Drive, Baton Rouge, LA 70806.

Gleaning Network—(includes Potato Project) Society of St. Andrew, State Rt. 615, P.O. Box 329, Big Island, VA 24526. 1-800-333-4597. Program to glean fresh produce from fields that would otherwise be plowed under.

Habitat for Humanity International—(also Global Village Work Camp) 121 Habitat Street, Americus, GA 31709. (800) 422-4828. Older teens can participate, and some projects include families with elementary children.

Heifer Project International—P.O. Box 808, Little Rock, AR 72203. Assists poor families in rural areas throughout the world to produce more food and income for themselves with improved livestock. A curriculum (notebook of stories, activities, and information) is now available from Heifer Project International. You can give amounts of money for specific animals.

Mountain TOP—2704 Twelfth Ave. S., Nashville, TN 37204. (615) 298-1575. A ministry to disadvantaged people in Tennessee. They do have some families participate in fall weekend events and are in talking stages about more involved family opportunities.

National Arbor Day Foundation—100 Arbor Ave., Nebraska City, NE 68410. (402) 474-5655. Planting trees to improve our world.

Potato Project—P.O. Box 329, State Rt. 615, Big Island, VA 24526. (804) 299-5956. This project salvages vegetables left in the fields after commercial pickers have finished. Because the picking is done through volunteer labor, the foods can be delivered to the hungry for 1 cent per serving. You may purchase coloring books to advertise the project. Families sometimes participate in this project.

Presbyterian Hunger Program—Room 3207, 100 Witherspoon St., Louisville, KY 40202-1396.

Save Our Streams (SOS)—A part of the Izaak Walton League of America, 1401 Wilson Blvd., Level B, Arlington VA 22209. (703) 528-1818. From them you may learn how to conserve, maintain, protect, and restore the soil, forest, water, and other resources.

Shoeboxes for Liberty, Friends of the Americas—912 N. Forest Drive, Baton Rouge, LA 70806. Send for guidelines for boxes to pack for those in need.

Trevor's Campaign (blankets for homeless)—Trevor's Place, 1624 West Popular street, Philadelphia, PA 19130. (215) 236-4660. This campaign was begun by a young boy who saw homeless people on TV and wanted to help.

Trinity Braille Ministry—Trinity United Methodist Church, 3104 W. Glendale Ave., Phoenix, AZ 85051.

All-volunteer group that prepares braille copies of selected United Methodist church-school literature.

United Church of Christ—Office for Church in Society, 700 Prospect Ave., Cleveland, OH 44115-1100.

UMCOR (United Methodist Committee on Relief)—475 Riverside Drive, New York, NY 10115. Hot line for current needs and opportunities. 1-800-841-1235. Projects involving refugees, agriculture, disasters, forest reclamation, hunger, and more. Help by raising money for a particular project or through Volunteers in Mission (VIM). Families with teens have gone as part of work teams, even overseas. (Volunteer hot line 800-918-3100.)

United Thank Offering—Joint Commission on AIDS, Episcopal Church Center, 815 Second Ave., New York, NY 10017.

Additional Resources

☐ For more thoughts on stewardship, mission, and a practical review read several of the following books.

Ellis, Susan, Anne Weisbord, and Katherine Noyes. *Children as Volunteers*. Philadelphia: Energize, 1991.

Make a World of Difference: Creative Activities for Global Learning. New York: Friendship Press, 1990.

Halverson, Delia. *Helping Children Care for God's People* (suggestions are also appropriate for youth and adults). Nashville: Abingdon Press, 1994.

Harris, Edie, and Shirley Ramsey. *Sprouts*. Nashville: Discipleship Resources, 1995.

Javna, John, and the EarthWorks Group. *Fifty Simple Things Kids Can Do to Save the Earth*. Kansas City, Mo.: Andrews and McMeel, 1990.

Kemper, Kristen, ed. *Caring for God's World*. Prescott, Ariz.: Educational Ministries, 1991.

Lewis, Barbara. *A Kid's Guide to Social Action*. Minneapolis: Free Spirit Publishing, 1991.

McGinnis, James, and Kathleen McGinnis. *Parenting for Peace and Justice, Ten Years Later,* rev. ed. Maryknoll, N.Y.: Orbis Books, 1990.

Meagher, Laura. *Teaching Children About Global Awareness*. New York: Crossroad Publishing Co., 1991.

Newman, Gene, and Joni E. Tada. *All God's Children: Ministry with Disabled Persons,* rev. ed. Grand Rapids: Zondervan, 1993.

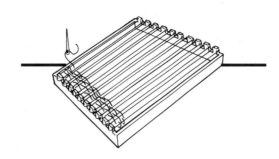

17 Learning Centers

Purpose: To explore ways that center learning may take place with adults, children, and youth, and to plan such centers.

Many people fear trying learning centers because they are afraid of losing control of the class. However, when a classroom is properly set up with learning centers, and ground rules are established, the students usually respond in a positive manner.

Basically, a *learning center* (sometimes called an activity center or learning-activity station) is an area in the classroom where specific resources and information are provided to guide the students in one or more learning activities. There may be one center in a room, or multiple centers, and sometimes such a center is mobile and brought into the classroom at a designated time.

Children with reading skills and youth and adults can progress at learning centers with very little assistance. This is done with specific signs and instructions at each center, explaining just what is to be done. General instructions may be laminated and used over and over. Learning centers may also be used with young children when adult leaders assist.

The number of teachers and assistants needed depends on the number of students and their ages. Younger children will need more assistance as they begin a project. One of the advantages to a learning center is that once the arena is set up, little training or preparation is required of the assistants who help at the centers. Parents make great assistants here.

Together Time

It is important to plan some sort of together time for the class, even if you will use several centers. Community is essential in Christian education, since God made us with a need to relate to one another. If all of your students arrive at the same time, then a beginning together time may work well. If they arrive at different times, you may want to close with a together time. Some teachers like to plan a short period together at both the beginning and close of the lesson. Another option is a together time for sharing the primary story or scripture during the lesson.

If you have students arriving and leaving at different times, you may choose to come together at a specified time during the lesson. If you do this, explain to the students that they may leave their work at the center and return to their stations after the together time.

Strengths and Weaknesses

Strengths:

Learning center education
● offers choices while allowing for individual differences.

- develops self-motivated learning.
- allows each individual to be different, as God created us.
- builds relationships among students in smaller groups.
- allows students who have missed to catch up. (This is a real plus in classes where single parents have shared custody of children.)
- if planned well, allows more activity for the amount of space.
- provides variety for children.
- allows each student to move at his or her own pace.
- may be used with mixed ages in the same room, which sometimes encourages older students to help younger ones.

Weaknesses:

Learning center education
- usually requires more adult leaders, but many of these leaders can be brought in for short terms.
- requires concentrated blocks of preparation time, although total preparation time may not be greater over the entire teaching period.
- requires a room where centers can be left up from week to week or requires extra time to set up and take down each week.
- unless there is a system for checking which centers the learner has covered, the learner may miss some content necessary to complete the learning goals.

Preparing for Centers

A learning center approach may be used for special theme learning events or for weekly Sunday school classes. The following procedure will walk you through the steps of preparing centers with printed curriculum. If you are setting the centers up without curriculum, then you will need to decide the purpose and theme of the study and plan accordingly (see "Lesson Planning" on page 106).

Select a session (individual lesson) from your curriculum and follow these steps:

☐ Read through your curriculum. As you read, mark activities that you may adapt to learning centers. Think about the students, your adult workers, and the physical location.

☐ Rewrite the overall goal of the unit (series of lessons with one theme) and the session in your own words. You may eventually return to using the curriculum's wording for your goal, but writing it in your own words will internalize the goal.

Unit goal:

_____

_____

_____

Session goal:

_____

_____

_____

☐ Using the activity suggestions in your curriculum, think about various kinds of centers for the session. Some may be required of each student, and some may be optional. Remember the learning styles of your students. (See "Multiple Intelligences," page 42.) Set up centers only for the activities you select.

AV center
This center can use various audiovisual resources. It may be pictures, audio recordings, film strips, or videos. Young children will need to have a large green dot-sticker on the play button and a large red dot-sticker on the stop button in order to handle the equipment without help.

Reading center
In this center you can display a variety of books that relate to the subject being studied. Be sure to change them about and make the center fresh. If you have some books that are real favorites, you might leave them in this center and encourage students who have finished other work to read them. Rocking chairs or comfortable floor pillows are popular here.

Creative writing center
You will either need a table or clipboards for this center. If the assignment is to write about a specific thing, such as God's gift of smell, then you can help the creative process

by displaying items relating to that subject, such as different scents, some good and some bad. Of course you will need whatever writing tools and paper your students are comfortable with. It might even be a computer, for some children!

Art center

Art comes in many forms, so vary the different mediums. Sometimes use paints, sometimes markers, and be sure to give opportunity for use of clay. Even adults enjoy clay after they get over the initial shock of being asked to use it! Many of your "crafty" activities will fall in this area. One word of precaution: Do not use food items for crafts (such as beans, rice, etc.). This sends the student a double message: There are people starving for a few spoons of rice, but it's O.K. to use it for crafts. Such use will dampen the impact of your Christian message of caring for others.

Music center

This center can have audio tapes of sing-along music, but one of the best ways to use such a center is to help children be creative with simple instruments, such as the Autoharp, piano or keyboard, and rhythm instruments. They can even make their own musical instruments out of pie tins (put together with stones inside), oatmeal box or tin can drums, rhythm sticks, and bells fastened to elastic to go around the wrist or ankle.

Puzzle/game center

Your curriculum may include board games or a set of cards related to the subject. This would be the place for such games. All puzzles and games should relate to the subject being studied. The one exception would be games that help students learn to use their Bible, because this skill is necessary for all their work.

Reflection center

In today's rushed schedule, we seldom have opportunity for reflection. This is one center that will be good to have at all times. It gives a student permission to get away from pressures and quietly reflect. It should be comfortable, and there may be some devotional materials. You will have instructions in some curriculum for quiet thinking and perhaps reflection on some subject. The student may even spend time in reflection and then move to another center to respond in some creative way on the reflection time. Some children's classes have such a center as a small loft, so as to have work space below. This is one center that should be used by one student at a time, unless it is large enough for more than one student to have private space.

☐ Look closely at the suggested activities in your curriculum and select those that can be used at these centers:

Audiovisual center

_____

_____

Reading center

_____

_____

Creative writing center

_____

_____

Art center

_____

_____

Music center

_____

_____

Puzzle/game center

_____

_____

Reflection center

_____

_____

_____

☐ Decide whether centers will be the primary activity of the session or only one part, with students taking turns at the center. Just how will the center or centers fit into your schedule?

_____

_____

☐ Map your classroom, including the location of each center and the location for a together time.

☐ Write clear instructions for each activity. If instructions may be found in the student booklet or handout or another piece of material, be careful to note this.

Materials	Where Stored?

_____

_____

☐ Make an "I did it" sheet or chart for each student. The sheet should have a place for the student's name, the station name, and the activity completed.

☐ Provide each student with a box, large envelope, or folder in which to store unfinished work.

☐ After each session, evaluate the stations, deciding how they might be changed, eliminated, or replaced.

_____

_____

☐ Evaluate the progress of the students, individually.

_____

_____

☐ Plan a large sign or poster that will create excitement and tell the students something about the overall theme. This poster may be made by students at the art center at the beginning of the first session.

_____

_____

☐ List materials you will need for each center and where they will be stored.

☐ Check station supplies periodically and replenish as needed.

☐ Offer a prayer about the session and ask for guidance in upcoming sessions.[1]

_____

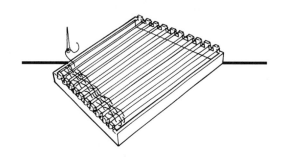

18 Lesson Planning

Purpose: To develop a method of lesson planning that increases effectiveness in teaching and also deepens the teacher's spirituality.

Most of us who have taught for a while have experienced not having time to do any planning. We grabbed the lesson book as we ran out the door and looked it over on the way to the church (unless we were driving). On such occasions we thank God for being able to draw from our past teaching experience and pray for the guidance of the Holy Spirit.

This lack of planning certainly does not bring about meaningful lessons, even when we have a printed curriculum to follow. The students can sense our lack of preparation. We have so little time in the classroom, it is important that we make it prime time.

Planning with Curriculum

One of the important things to remember about curriculum is that we do not teach it. We *use* it. *We teach persons and use curriculum* as a tool or a guide. Most curriculum have more suggestions for activities than the average teacher will have time to use. This gives the teacher opportunity to consider the learners when selecting just what to include.

In most curriculum there are also additional activities that may be substituted for an activity that does not seem to be appropriate for your students. Estimate the time each activity will require, and plan an extra one or two activities in case you have extra time. Consider which activity you will drop if you run short of time.

Be sure to experiment with any activity that you have not tried before, by creating a sample. If you haven't already tried it, you will have difficulty helping your students with the project.

Weekly Preparation Plan

Without a routine, it is easy to put off planning, day after day, until Saturday night, only to discover that you have no craft sticks and the craft stores are closed! The best lesson preparation begins early in the week, giving your mind time to mull the ideas during those days. This allows God opportunity to mold the plans to your particular class and style.

☐ Devise a weekly plan for preparing your lesson. Try the plan on the next page and adapt it to your style and situation. There are seven sections; the plan works well when you follow one section each day.

Plan for Preparation

*P*ray for your students and for your preparation. Read and meditate on the scripture.

*R*ead the materials and rewrite the goals in your own words.

*E*xamine the lesson plan and select what you will use.

*P*lan the schedule and who is responsible for what.

*A*rrange the room, collect supplies, and make any samples.

*R*eview the scripture and plans.

*E*njoy teaching! Afterward, consider what happened during the session that was positive and what part of the session might have been done better.

Lesson Checklist

As you prepare for your next lesson, use this checklist.

☐ Is there something that will catch the student's attention immediately?

☐ Are the activities appropriate for the age level and individuals?

☐ Is there a mix of activities?

    Active and quiet times _____

    Verbal and mental _____

    Individual and group _____

☐ Are there transition times?

☐ How is the Bible used? Are there opportunities to *feel into, meet with,* and *respond out of* the Bible? (See page 137.)

☐ Does the lesson relate to the students' everyday lives?

☐ Are the needs of each student considered? What about the person who demands special attention or dominates the discussion? What about the one who never contributes?

☐ Do you have more planned than you expect to use, and do you know what to drop if time runs short?

☐ Is there a closure to the session?[1]

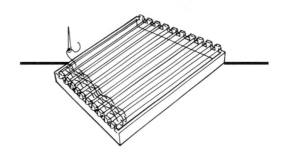

19 Positive Classroom Atmosphere

Purpose: To create a better learning atmosphere and develop tools for handling situations that might arise.

The atmosphere in your classroom makes a lot of difference in the cooperative learning of your students. The physical surroundings of your classroom create the first impression. Students learn better when they are comfortable. Whether you teach children, youth, or adults, the character of your classroom sets the mood for learning.

Analyze the Atmosphere

☐ Physically, approach your classroom as if you were a new student. If necessary, stoop or kneel down in order to have the same eye level that your student would have. What catches your eye?

_____

_____

_____

_____

_____

☐ Where is the focal point as you enter the room?

_____

_____

_____

_____

_____

_____

☐ What can you do to make that focal point more inviting?

_____

_____

_____

_____

☐ Is there clutter? How can you make better use of the storage you have or arrange for additional storage?

_____

_____

_____

_____

☐ Is the furniture appropriate for the age level, or are the students uncomfortable? How might that be adjusted?

_____

_____

_____

_____

☐ Is there too much furniture for the room? How might that be changed? (With children, consider removing some tables and chairs and providing a rug for sitting. Older students and adults can use clipboards instead of desks or tables.)

_____

_____

_____

_____

Take a Look at Your Schedule

Are you trying to get too much done in the amount of time you have? Remember that you do not have to accomplish everything that is laid out in your curriculum. You can also substitute methods of teaching, being sure to carry through on the same subject, theme, scripture, and so on.

☐ How might you expand or cut back your activities?

_____

_____

_____

_____

☐ Is there a balance of active and passive activities? What sort of change do you need to make in order to achieve a better balance?

_____

_____

_____

_____

_____

☐ What might you use for warning signals (word of mouth, music, flip of light switch)?

_____

_____

_____

_____

☐ Do the students know what to expect? How might you adjust your schedule? (Remember that students need a warning signal before completing their work and you must build transition time into your schedule.)

_____

_____

_____

_____

☐ Are you in the classroom with everything ready before the first student appears? Your preparation makes a lot of difference in how the lesson starts. If it's impossible for you to be there early, how might you set up ahead of time and whom might you ask to be there early to greet the students?

_____

_____

_____

_____

Look at Your Communication

We communicate not only with words, but also with actions, the clothing we wear, and our facial expressions. Look through a lesson in your curriculum and consider your students.

☐ If your students are young, what words or concepts are used that would be used differently for adults? (Remember that most children cannot understand abstract concepts.)

_____

_____

_____

☐ If your students are teenagers, what words in the curriculum are common expressions and are currently being used by them?

_____

_____

_____

_____

_____

_____

☐ If your students are adults, what words or concepts take for granted that the adult has prior understanding or is more mature in his or her faith than most of your students actually are?

_____

_____

_____

_____

_____

☐ Try to phrase your statements or comments in positive rather than negative terms. Reword the following as positive statements.

Negative	Positive
Don't all of you sit on the back row.	_____
Don't hit him with the stick!	_____
Don't drop the clay on the floor.	_____
It's not your turn to answer.	_____
Don't run in the hall.	_____
You're never here on time.	_____

☐ All students, no matter what the age, need affirmations. There is always something positive that you can say about someone, even if it is only the color of their clothing or telling them that their comment was an interesting way to make a statement. Consider several persons in your class and write some affirmations you might use with them. Especially consider any "trouble-makers" or difficult students you may have.

need to be most conscious of?

_____

_____

_____

Name	Affirmation
_____	_____
_____	_____
_____	_____
_____	_____
_____	_____
_____	_____

☐ Stand in front of a mirror and practice giving any information, instructions, or a story from an upcoming lesson. What sort of facial expressions would be most appropriate?

_____

_____

_____

_____

_____

_____

_____

_____

_____

_____

☐ If you work with children, ask another adult to stand in front of you while you squat down to the child's eye level and look up at the adult. Young children draw an adult's face with a round circle, two eyes, a mouth, and two dots for the nose. This is their view of us! What do you see?

_____

_____

_____

☐ For the next twenty-four hours, pay close attention to the way that you stand, sit, and walk. Do you transfer excitement about what you are doing? Remember that crossing your arms gives a hostile and unapproachable appearance. What actions do you

_____

_____

Set Guidelines (or Covenants) for Your Classroom

These are important for classes of all ages. However, the class needs to have ownership in the guidelines. Think through the following ways that you can lead your class in developing guidelines.

☐ With children and youth, talk together about ways that you can best work together and treat each person as a child of God. Then help the students consolidate the ideas into several positive statements about the way that the class will act and post them on the wall. What are some suggestions the students might have? (Example: We will take turns speaking.)

_____

_____

_____

_____

_____

_____

☐ What are some consequences that might come about when the guidelines aren't carried out? Be sure to include these in the guidelines (such as a warning, removal or conference, parent contact, joint conference with pastor, parent, teacher, and child).

_____

_____

_____

☐ Adults also need guidelines. These might include an allotment of time for coffee and conversation, announcements, and so on. They might also include contacting persons who miss class and following up on members who are ill. What are some "understood" guidelines that your class already has?

_____

_____

_____

_____

_____

☐ What are some additional ones you might consider?

_____

_____

_____

_____

_____

_____

Positive Discipline

The word _discipline_ actually comes from the word _disciple_. When we act as a disciple of someone, we shape our behavior so that it follows the direction or leadership of the other person. This is done on a voluntary basis, not by dictatorship. Consequently, in order to help our students *self*-discipline their good behavior pattern, we must devise situations in which they will want to follow our lead. We want them to take the rules, even helping to establish them, and make them internal. Students will follow internal rules voluntarily, but external rules must usually be enforced with external punishment. We want to create in our students a desire to develop affirmative behavior.

In the circumstances of today's Sunday school, this is a challenge. One of the first steps toward this is to build a positive group relationship within your class. Do not expect this to happen overnight.

☐ How many hours will a teacher in your school system have with his or her students by the end of the first week in the fall?

_____

_____

_____

☐ How many weeks will it take for you to have the same number of hours with your weekly class?

_____

_____

☐ Which students in your class come regularly unless they are sick?

_____

_____

_____

_____

_____

_____

☐ Which students in your class routinely spend one or two weeks with a parent living elsewhere?

_____

_____

_____

_____

_____

_____

These facts only point out the importance of group building and the necessity of your consistent attendance as a teacher. Group building is hard to achieve when teachers trade off, week by week. Team teaching, where all team teachers are in the classroom most weeks, makes for a much more cohesive group. A class routine then develops that can be depended on. You, as teacher, know how the student acted last week, and the student can build confidence in you.

Sometimes we have students who consistently cause trouble. These situations need individual attention.

☐ Practice talking privately with the student in this manner:

1. Take the child or youth away from the class and name the unacceptable action.
2. Ask the student to tell you in his or her own words what he or she did wrong.
3. Allow a few seconds of thinking time, while showing your disapproval with facial expression.
4. Smile and hug or touch the student on the shoulder and say, "Your behavior was not good, but you are good. I love you, and God loves you. I know you can do better."[1]

Try this approach several times. If all your efforts fail, arrange for a conference with the parent. In some cases you may want to ask the pastor to sit in on the conference. Be sure that your anger has cooled, and plan some positive statements about the child to sandwich the negative. Ask the parent for insights into how to handle the situation. If the child is on medication during the week, ask that the medication also be given on Sunday.

And above all else, pray for your class and love, love, love each individual student!

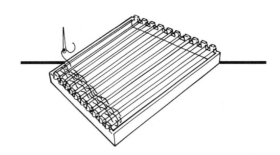

20 prayer in the classroom

purpose: To understand appropriate use of prayer according to the age and situation in the classroom and to develop skills for creating favorable conditions for prayer.

Most of us recognize the importance of having prayer as a part of our class experience, but often it becomes routine or we simply tack it on at the beginning or end of the lesson. If we truly believe in prayer as our opportunity to communicate with God, then it should be an integral part of each time we come together as Christians. It should also be a part of our planning and preparation.

☐ For information on the elements of prayer (ACTS, as follows), read page 52.

☐ Read Matthew 6:9-13 and identify the sections that are:

A doration
_____

C onfession
_____

T hanksgiving
_____

S upplication
_____

Age Level Understanding

Even very young children can pray, and I believe that they do it more often than we realize. They just don't know how to label it. When a child is upset and sits and talks to a dog or stuffed animal, it is a form of prayer. Because the child's abstract thinking has not developed, the concrete presence of the animal or toy helps to make it more real. The child is searching for an opportunity to share concern and to be heard and understood by a being more powerful than those around him or her.

The following suggestions are guides to help you understand how to approach prayer with students of varying ages. You will find that these age guides do not always hold true, because some children have had more opportunity to experience prayer than others. If you teach an older class that is unaccustomed to praying, you may need to begin with prayers for an earlier age level and build their comfort in prayer.

Nursery
● Associate prayer with good things.
● Pray prayers of thanksgiving and praise.

- Pray with the child in the manner of talking to God. Begin to build the relationship with God.
- Use simple language: "you" and "your," not "thee," "thou," and "thine."
- No particular body position is necessary.
- The child need not always close eyes.
- Giving thanks for food after eating makes more sense to a child of this age.

Kindergarten
- Provide some opportunities for prayer.
- Pray spontaneous prayers. "Talk" to God.
- Prayer can be two to five short sentences of everyday speech. Pray what the child understands.
- Religion is private; prayer is not a time to show off. Be cautious of asking the child to pray before guests.
- Evening prayers: Talk over happy times of the day, kindnesses, how God helped—then pray.
- Begin requests for help: "Help me to remember to cross the street carefully . . . to take turns . . . to help others." Pray for someone else, such as: "Help the doctor to help Johnny."
- Begin to distinguish between asking Daddy for toys and asking God to help us take turns. God works through people for physical needs.

Grades 1-3
- Continue praise and thanksgiving prayers.
- Encourage the child to compose his or her own written prayers.
- Create litany prayers together.
- Give opportunities for sentence prayers *after* discussion of what we are thankful for—don't pray "in turn" or force the child to pray.
- Acknowledge the need for forgiveness.
- Encourage prayers asking for help, making them more specific than before.

Grades 4-6
- Encourage personal and private worship.
- Provide devotional materials.
- Help the child to appreciate prayers in formal worship.
- Study prayers in the hymnal for special occasions and prayer hymns.
- Continue prayer as a close relationship with God.
- Encourage growth so that this relationship with God is there when the child is more independent.

Youth
- Continue to encourage personal and private worship.
- Expand use of formal, printed prayers and learn about the authors.
- Include intercessory prayers in your class plans.
- Recognize and study prayers of anger and frustration in the Psalms.
- Prayers for guidance will help youth during difficult times.[1]

Adults
- In brief conversational style, use everyday words in your own prayers. This helps the students know that they can pray very naturally.
- Allow brief periods of silence during a prayer for private thoughts.
- If the class is not accustomed to praying aloud, begin by using general discussion about thanksgivings, prayer concerns, and so on. Then simply close with a very brief sentence such as, "You have heard these things we've shared, our God. Thank you for your care. Amen."
- If you would like to have someone else pray during the class period, ask them privately ahead of time, and let them know that you want them to pray only if they will feel comfortable doing so. Never put someone on the spot, unless you know that the person is accustomed to praying aloud spontaneously.
- Consider guided meditative prayer as a way of helping adults think through their prayers. (See page 118.)

Setting the Stage

There are many opportunities for spontaneous prayer in the classroom, but sometimes it will be helpful to plan opportunities for your students to grow in their prayer life. Praying doesn't happen only when we bow our heads and close our eyes. Praying can also happen as we think through problems, ideas, and situations. Sometimes this is done with mental images, and sometimes it is more helpful to do it visually or by actually making something.

☐ List some methods that might be used to help students think through their prayers. Include such things as murals, clay, choosing from various pictures, body movements, singing, and so forth.

_____

_____

_____

_____

_____

_____

_____

_____

_____

Name-calling
Unfriendly, unloving
Hurting, painful, distressing
I forgive and love.
Amen.

Prayer Poems

Poems simply express our thoughts in a form that uses fewer words. Creating prayer poems does not need to be a literary work of art. Sometimes the prayer may rhyme, but more often we simply use short sentences or phrases.

One of the easiest forms to use is the *cinquain* (sin-cane) poem, which has only five lines. See the example above and write one below.

Movement Prayers

When we incorporate movement into our prayers, we are loving God with our whole selves, with body as well as heart and mind. Movement may be a part of the prayers that the class creates, or it may be adapted to printed prayers. Young children can participate in very concrete movements. Older children, youth, and adults can understand movement that symbolizes a feeling or attitude. Some of our prayers from the early church heritage are more meaningful to children when we add movement to them. Prayer hymns are easily adapted to movement prayers.

As you decide which movements to use, remember that you do not need a movement for every word or phrase. Make the movements simple. The movement prayer is not a performance, but a communication between the participant and God. Never "practice" the prayer; always pray it. Welcome different ways of expressing the words. Here are some possible movements that may come out of your group:

#1 One-word title or subject   _____

#2 Two words that tell about the
   subject (a phrase or separate words)   _____ _____

#3 Three action words (verbs or "ing" words)
   or a phrase about the subject   _____ _____ _____

#4 Four words or a phrase telling of
   feelings about the subject   _____ _____ _____ _____

#5 The subject word again, or synonym, or Amen   _____

Approaching God	*Step forward, head held high*
Praise	*Uplifted head, upward movement of arms*
Receive gifts; Holy Spirit	*Head bowed, arms curved over head, fingertips touching head*
Communicating	*Hand movement from lips upward as if to God and outward as if to others*
Heaven and earth	*One arm stretched up and in front; other arm stretched down and behind*
Whole universe	*With right hand, circle left to right*
Springtime; new birth	*Hands together at chest and then moving upward like sprouts coming from earth*
Fellowship	*Arms across neighbors' shoulders*
Unity	*Clasping neighbors' hands*
Rejecting evil	*Hands to side, lowered and pushing back*
Repentance	*Kneeling, looking up, bowed head*
Amen	*Head bowed, arms relaxed*[2]

☐ Select a prayer hymn or printed prayer and write down actions that might accompany the words.

_____

_____

☐ Look at Psalm 100 and select parts for a leader, two groups, and the entire class to read.

☐ Choose another psalm and do the same thing, selecting some verses for individuals to read.

☐ Write a sentence in each space below, thanking God for something.

Litany Prayers or Choral Readings

Litanies and choral readings are done antiphonally (first one group or individual, and then another). The simplest way to plan this is to divide your class into two or three groups. You may also include some individual readings at places. Or you may want to select the phrases that lend heavier or darker feelings and have them spoken by the deeper voices, or the group as a whole, and lighter phrases by individuals with higher voices.

Thanks Be to God

God has given us many wonderful things.

_____

For this we thank you, O God.

_____

For this we thank you, O God.

_____

For this we thank you, O God.

_____

You have just created a simple litany prayer. To use this in a classroom, print the form for the prayer on large paper or board and ask different students to give you sentences to put in the blanks. Ask each one to remember which line you wrote the student's sentence on, or place their names beside their sentences. As leader, you will read the first sentence. Those who contributed will read their sentences. And everyone will read the response that is in italics. If the students are too young to read, tell them what the response sentence is. Even though they cannot read, they can remember what they told you to write.

☐ You might also create a litany prayer on the subject of the lesson with older children, teens, and adults. The sentences might be:

Times you find it hard to do what is right.
Response: Psalm 86:11*a*

Persons and situations the students would like the class to remember in prayer.
Response: Psalm 10:17

_____

_____

Prayer Journal

The words *journal* and *diary* have been interchanged in recent years. The prayer journal is quite different from a diary. Where a diary focuses on what happened and to whom, the prayer journal focuses on who and wherefore. It reflects on events, needs, problems, and joys as they relate to God. It might be written as a "Dear God" letter. It will often include a lot of questioning thoughts.

If you use journaling in the classroom, be sure it is understood that this is private, and no one, not even the teacher, will read the journal unless asked to. Some teen and adult classes find it helpful to spend the first ten minutes of each class period journaling about how God has been a part of their lives in the past week. When the students reread their own journals, there will be indications of their faith growth.

☐ Read the suggestion for a prayer pattern that uses a journal on page 55 and then spend a week journaling at a given time each day. At the end of the week, write

your reactions to the experience here.

_____

_____

_____

Guided Meditative Prayer

If students have little experience in prayer, then a guided meditation will help them think through their prayers. This also helps you to direct their prayers in a specific direction for your lesson. Work through this example of a meditative prayer yourself. Then use the suggestions that follow to create your own meditative prayer.

● Close your eyes and imagine that you are at a place you enjoy going to alone. Visualize something about that place.
● Relax and listen to your slow breathing, in and out.
● Think of the very center of your soul. Ask God to come into your soul, breathing deeply as you feel God become a part of you.
● Share any concerns you have with God.
● Release those concerns to God, knowing that God will see you through them, even if they are not resolved immediately.
● Tell God of the joys in your life, and rejoice with God over those joys.
● Listen to what God may be telling you.
● Now allow all else to leave your mind, and simply "look and love" God.
● When you are ready, close your prayer with "Amen."

● Think of a quiet, calm place that your students might be familiar with.

_____

_____

☐ How can you describe that place to help the student visualize it?

_____

_____

☐ Close your eyes and think of the part inside yourself that laughs when you are happy and cries when you are sad. Think of the part of you that loves and that feels good when you do something for others. How can you describe that part of you?

_____

_____

_____

This might be called your soul. Children may better understand it as "the really-really me."

☐ What words might you use to guide meditation when studying these subjects?

Creation

_____

_____

Concern for others

_____

_____

Jesus' life

_____

_____

Choices

_____

_____

Family

_____

_____

Forgiveness

_____

_____

_____

☐ Plan words for a meditative prayer in your class. Remember that young children will have a very short attention span, and so only two or three sentences is a sufficient length for them.

_____

_____

Additional Resources

☐ Review several of these resources and consider which ones will be helpful as you assist your students in building their prayer life.

Alive Now (adult devotional magazine). The Upper Room (P.O. Box 189, Nashville, TN 37202-9929).

Devo'Zine (youth devotional magazine). The Upper Room (P.O. Box 189, Nashville, TN 37202-9929).

Griggs, Donald. *Praying and Teaching the Psalms.* Nashville: Abingdon Press, 1984.

Halpin, Marlene. *Puddles of Knowing* (planning prayer experiences for children). Dubuque, Iowa: William C. Brown, 1984.

Halverson, Delia. *How Do Our Children Grow?* (chap. 6 on prayer). Nashville: Abingdon Press, 1993.

————. *Teaching Prayer in the Classroom.* Nashville: Abingdon Press, 1989 (out of print currently, but may be ordered through "Books on Demand," 615-749-6311).

Ingram, Kristen Johnson. *Family Worship Through the Year.* Valley Forge, Pa.: Judson Press, 1984.

Jones-Pendergast, Kevin, ed. *Letters to God from Teenagers.* Cincinnati: St. Anthony Messenger Press, 1979.

Kichenburger, James. *Fun Devotions for Parents and Teenagers.* Loveland, Colo.: Group Publishing, 1990.

Koch, Carl, ed. *Dreams Alive: Prayers by Teenagers.* Winona, Minn.: St. Marys, 1991.

Neinast, Helen, and Thomas C. Ettinger. *What About God Now That You're Off to College? A Prayer Guide.* Nashville: Upper Room, 1992.

Pockets (a children's devotional periodical). Upper Room (P.O. Box 189, Nashville, TN 37202-9929).

Smith, Judy Gattis. *Teaching Children About Prayer* (five-session study for elementary children). Prescott, Ariz.: Educational Ministries, 1988.

Swanson, Steve. *Faith Prints: Youth Devotions for Every Day of the Year.* Minneapolis: Augsburg Fortress, 1985.

Teach Us to Pray (grades 2–6 elective unit: 6 basic 1-hour sessions with suggestions for expanding sessions. Teacher/student books). Nashville: Graded Press, 1985.

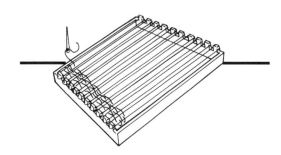

21 selecting curriculum for Adults

Purpose: To recognize the needs of your class and explore curriculum that will help you meet those needs.

Adult class members are more diverse than we often realize. They have varied needs and varied biblical knowledge. They are diverse in their interests and in their preferred ways of learning. For this reason, most churches have at least two adult classes. There is no way that one class can meet everyone's needs.

Classes tend to develop around homogeneous groups. Warren J. Hartman, in his book *Five Audiences,* approaches the following groupings in the church, based on beliefs, attitudes, expectations of the church, and other characteristics.

Fellowship—They enjoy the use of media, seek stability in teachers, enjoy informal discussion, place high value on relationships, have no strong institutional ties, desire curriculum relevant to them today.

Traditionalists—They are Bible-oriented, beliefs are important, usually enjoy dated curriculum and regular teachers, prefer lectures, are loyal to church and Sunday school class, enjoy traditional classroom patterns and resist changes. (*Neo-traditionalists,* those who have recently returned to the faith, share theological views with Traditionalists, enjoy Bible or spiritual formation curriculum, look for biblical and theological mentors, are highly influenced by books and magazines, and often switch from one church to another searching for a class or study to meet their current needs.)

Study—They have supervisory and professional careers, are tolerant to positions other than their own, study Christian faith and life applications, are highly ecumenical, prefer to choose their teacher who is a colearner, like good teaching aids, enjoy curriculum relevant to today, relate well to others.

Social Action Group—They have people-centered and service-oriented careers, faith is a private matter, place more importance on social action than spiritual disciplines, view church and class as launching pad for action and want the teacher to help explore needs they might meet, have little patience with those who do not share their concerns.

Multiple Interest Group—They entertain views half-way between other groups, usually combining fellowship with another area, make up the majority of congregation, respect others' views, are comfortable with a wide variety of teaching methods and curricula.[1]

☐ Consider your class and the characteristics just listed. Which group best defines your class members?

_____

_____

_____

☐ Review the characteristics of the different generations on pages 23-27. Which generations are represented in your class?

_____

_____

_____

☐ Is the class predominantly from one generation? Which one?

_____

Goals

In setting goals for your class study, consider both the needs of your class members and the mission statement of your church. This will help the class to integrate with the congregation.

☐ Read the mission statement of your church. What are the key words?

_____

_____

_____

☐ Consider the makeup of your class. What is happening in their lives? What problems and pressures are members facing now?

_____

_____

_____

☐ Periodically you may want to prepare a written Adult Study Interest Survey for the class. A suggested survey form can be found in *Leading Adult Learners* (Abingdon Press, 1995), page 77.

☐ What words describe the ways that you hope your class members will grow in the upcoming year?

_____

_____

_____

_____

☐ Begin to form **purpose statements.** You might include growth in:

● biblical and theological understanding in everyday life situations.
● knowledge of the Bible.
● spiritual formation and communication with God.
● appreciation for the church's history and mission.
● living the faith and sharing it with others each day.

_____

_____

_____

_____

☐ Set specific **measurable goals** such as:

● Learn about the symbols found in our sanctuary.
● Practice ways to mention God without sounding pious.
● Recognize opportunities for spontaneous worship of God.

_____

_____

_____

_____

Consider the Calendar

Both the yearly and church calendars can give you ideas for possible study. If our Christian life is to be lived out in life every day, then it is appropriate to study in the context of what's going on in our daily lives. You will find suggestions for subjects developed around calendars on pages 54-57 of *Leading Adult Learners.*

Look at Resources

There are several places that you can find study resources. Be sure to check out these possibilities:

- your church library or your pastor's resource shelf.
- a Christian or denominational curriculum catalog.
- a church or denominational audiovisual lending library.
- inspirational or self-help books from the public library or bookstores.

Note: If you select something other than a church or denominational resource, be sure that you check with your education committee or pastor for approval.

Publicize Plans

Adults will make a greater effort to attend if they know that it is a subject that they are interested in. You should find ways to publicize lesson topics within your class and also throughout the church. Some church newsletters include a page specifically for adult classes to announce the subject matter of forthcoming lessons.

☐ Make a list of the subjects and dates for the class members.

_____

_____

_____

As you complete your curriculum plan, check these items:

☐ Have you considered the class members' interests and needs?

☐ Does the study agree with your church's mission statement?

☐ Is the material theologically consistent with your church?

☐ Is the study built on a biblical foundation?

☐ Will the study help students grow in their spiritual lives?

☐ Does the study encourage students to investigate their own beliefs?

☐ Will the study make a difference in the way that the students live their everyday lives?

☐ Make the information available for the newsletter or bulletin.

Additional Resources

Murray, Dick. *Teaching the Bible to Adults and Youth.* Nashville: Abingdon Press, 1993.
Osmer, Richard Robert. *Teaching for Faith.* Louisville: Westminster/John Knox, 1992.

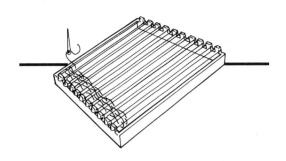

22 Taking the Maze Out of Your Room

Purpose: To become aware of the many opportunities to teach by using the various parts of the classroom.

Have you ever walked into a room, only to find yourself wishing you had never opened the door? What does this statement tell you about the welcoming atmosphere of your classroom? The environment of your room sends a message about just how important the students are and the importance of what goes on in that room. Even young children can receive these hidden messages. There are some elements of a room that are important for all age-level classrooms. All rooms should be or have:

Children Under Three

Rooms for *children under three* give varying first experiences in the church. We want these experiences to be comfortable, safe, and happy. Consider these:

Threes, Fours, Fives

Rooms for *children three through five* need space for

bright and uncluttered
age-appropriate furnishings
space pictures at appropriate heights
clean, inviting, exciting
well-kept storage
worship or wonder center
chairs in semicircle or circle formation
where possible

both individual and group activity. Plan permanent centers for such activities as housekeeping, blocks, books, and art allowing children to move freely from one to another. Include a nature table and a place to play games. For working, several small tables are better than one

cleanliness	appropriate furniture (cribs, etc.)
cuddling corner	age-appropriate toys
individual play and learning places	divided doors (may open top half alone)
water tap in room	bright colors (except in sleeping areas)

large one, and consider pushing back all tables sometimes and using the floor. Include a rug or pillow corner for storytelling, singing, or conversation.

Early Elementary

Early elementary children can work in small groups, but often work side by side on the same project, helping each other along. Some permanent centers are still appropriate for this age, such as a book center, a listening and media center, and a nature center. Most children this age can learn to operate a tape player and simple filmstrip projector. Many of them can also use a VCR and a computer. Provide an area with children's Bible dictionaries, storybooks about Bible times, and other research resources appropriate for this age. These children are old enough to enjoy a puppet center and a collection of costumes for extemporaneous drama.

Older Elementary

Older elementary children enjoy many of the centers that early elementary children do. They can work on longer projects, and so sometimes your room may be set up for a large, continuing project for several weeks at a time. If your room doesn't allow space for study tables as well as open space for group activities, consider purchasing inexpensive clipboards or plywood lap boards for each student. These may be painted by each student and taken home by the student at the end of the year or saved from year to year.

Youth

Spend some time in settings other than the church with your youth. By visiting with them at school, for example, you can discover what makes your group unique. Contrary to public opinion, youth will respond to nice furniture and an uncluttered room, if they have ownership in it. They do enjoy a casual atmosphere that does not remind them of school, and they prefer to sit in a circle rather than rows. A circle or semicircle arrangement of chairs helps youth to be more attentive and enriches the atmosphere of community. They enjoy clipboards or tables, but don't spend the whole time at tables; use a variety of activities.

Use bright posters on the wall. You might even consider painting a mural or time line on the wall during class time and using this as a learning tool.

Adults

The setup of adult classrooms depends on the individual class preference. Generally adults learn best in an informal setting; however, many adults have spent most of their lives sitting in straight rows. If a class has a tradition of assembly-type seating, you may need to experiment with groups of two or three talking together at times and feel the class out before moving to a more informal setting.

Because adult classes so often seem to carry on in the same way they have for years, they can easily get into a rut. There is comfort in the familiar, but if we become too comfortable, we are not challenged to break out into new modes of thought. This same sort of comfort status also allows an adult class to overlook clutter and not recognize an uncaring attitude about a classroom. They see it so often that they tend to overlook the surroundings as they concentrate on more immediate things. This, however, is a negative signal for a new person coming into the classroom. It indicates that you are not current with your teaching and subject matter. It says, "This is the same old thing we've done forever. Nothing new or exciting goes on here."

Make an eye-catching sign for your door. Keep a current bulletin board with items of interest for the class members as well as pictures of past events. The name tags tell a visitor that you want them to know your name, thereby signaling that you welcome them. Make name tags obvious. Provide a focal point or worship center in keeping with the subject of the lesson. A focal point tells visitors and regulars alike that the lesson is well planned and of importance to you. Change it often.

Any Age

No matter what the age, an orderly, bright, clean room enhances learning. Use the highest wattage bulbs permissible in your light fixtures, and be sure they all work. Paint the walls a light, neutral color, and cover windows sparingly or use a simple wallpaper or stenciled border around the windows. Remember that walls are good teaching tools and any decorations need to be changed according to your lesson theme. Use bedsheets or large papers to cover distracting areas in shared-space classrooms. Carpet or "sit-upon" carpet squares make the floor a good teaching tool also. Staple large sheets of construction paper or plain wallpaper to unsightly bulletin boards to brighten up the room.

Small changes will stimulate excitement in your room. Remember, however, that too much of anything is distracting. Frequent changes with fewer items help children to focus. This is particularly true for people—children, youth, and adults—with learning disabilities.

Chairs arranged in a circle or semicircle contribute to a sense of community.

Ways to Use a Room

Rooms may be tools in teaching, and can be as effective as markers and newsprint. This is part of the unwritten curricula that we often ignore.

☐ Visit other classrooms in your church building and arrange to look at classrooms in other churches. On the blanks at right, list different ways to use these parts of your classroom for teaching.

☐ Take thirty minutes during a time when no one is in your room to fill out the form "Room Check":

Hallways near your room

_____ _____
_____ _____

Doors

_____ _____
_____ _____

Walls

_____ _____
_____ _____

Ceilings

_____ _____
_____ _____

Windows

_____ _____
_____ _____

Furniture

_____ _____
_____ _____

Centers

_____ _____
_____ _____

Bulletin boards

_____ _____
_____ _____

Chalkboards

_____ _____
_____ _____

Unique storage possibilities

_____ _____
_____ _____

125

Room Check

1. As you approach the room, how can you tell who meets here?

_____

_____

2. As you enter the room, stand or squat at the eye level of your students who meet here. What do you see?

_____

_____

_____

Is there something that would make you (at the age of your student) want to come into the room? What?

_____

_____

_____

Is the room light? _____ dark? _____
What bright colors are in the room?_____

Are the pictures at the eye level of the students?_____

3. What in the room gives a hint of the subject to be taught this Sunday?

_____

What outside the door gives this information?

_____

4. Sit in the chairs. How do they feel? Can you see well?

_____

5. Is there anything outdated that is still in the room? what?

_____

6. Is there clutter in the room? How can you arrange additional storage or make better use of what you have?

_____

_____

7. Is there too much furniture or poorly arranged furniture to allow space for *active* learning? Can tables be removed and students use the floor or clipboards? How might you adjust this?

_____

_____

_____

8. Make any other notations that might make your room more learner friendly.

_____

_____

_____

☐ Considering this form, look for ways you can make a difference in your classroom by using the form that follows.

Ways I Can Improve the Room	Target Date	Date Accomplished
Just outside the room, identify it with a sign and information on the class.		
Place pictures, etc. at eye level of students.		
Arrange for more light in the room.		
Use bright colors.		
Add _____ as a focal point for the subject being taught.		
Go through materials and store or discard those not needed.		
Rearrange furniture for better teaching.		
Other ideas		

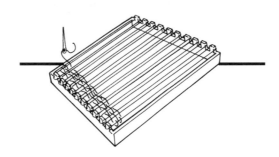

23 Using Questions in Teaching

Purpose: To sharpen your skills of asking questions so that more effective learning takes place.

Questions are good teaching tools if they are worded correctly. Questions should stimulate thought for the student. Sometimes we use questions to introduce a subject or scripture. Or we might use them to help students think of how the scripture might be applied to their own lives, or what they might do in a given situation. Questions may also encourage discussion, if they demand more than a yes or no answer.

In Christian education we focus on helping persons learn *how* to think rather than *what* to think. We use questions to motivate students to think on their own. We can never teach persons exactly *what* to do in every situation, but we can help them gain the skills to think through each situation and arrive at a solution that would be in keeping with Jesus' teachings.

One thing to keep in mind as you work with questions is that some people think while they talk, and some people form their thoughts *before* they talk. Don't be embarrassed by silence. What seems like a long silence to a teacher may be only a short time to students organizing their thoughts.

Youth and adults need to have clarifiers, persons who don't give them the answers but help them clarify their values and make choices. After we encourage brainstorming and their interpretation of values, we then help them to move toward a commitment. As teachers, we create the atmosphere. The Holy Spirit actually brings about the transformation.

And so it is important that questions more often become transformational than informational.

Jesus Used Questions in His Teaching

☐ Explore a time that Jesus used a question to lead into a story, by reading Luke 10:25-30.

☐ If your lesson called for the story of the time Jesus helped a multitude of hungry people, what question might you use to encourage the students to "feel into" the situation? What would make the students think about what it might have felt like to actually be on site? Word the question so that it demands more than a yes or no answer.

_____

_____

_____

☐ Read Mark 11:27-33 to discover a time that Jesus responded to a question by returning a question to the inquirer.

☐ If a student asked you, "Do miracles happen today?" what question could you pose to cause the student to dig into the concept? (Be more specific than simply saying, "What do you think?")

_____

_____

☐ Jesus sometimes asked his listener's opinion. Read Luke 13:10-17.

☐ What question could you pose that would cause your students to think deeper about how it would feel to be on the receiving end of a "put-down"?

_____

_____

_____

☐ Reword the following questions so that your students must dig deeper for their thoughts.

Do you believe in miracles?

_____

_____

_____

Do you believe in God?

_____

_____

Were the readings for this week's lesson difficult?

_____

_____

_____

Types of Questions

Recall

 To gather or call to mind certain information.
Example: What Hebrew meal did Jesus eat with his disciples?

Organize Data

 To describe, compare, or contrast data.
Example: What mileage in our city compares with the distance that Jesus traveled from Bethany to Jerusalem during Holy Week?

Analyze

 To explore an explanation or reasons related to a situation or action.
Example: Why do you think Judas arranged for the officials to arrest Jesus?

Judgment

 To make choices, connections, draw conclusions, and evaluate.
Example: Considering Jesus' cleansing of the Temple, should we sell items in the church?

Speculate

 To imagine and identify possibilities of situations.
Example: What would you have done if you had been a follower of Jesus and came upon a crowd in the street, only to discover that they were watching Jesus carry the cross?[1]

USING QUESTIONS IN TEACHING

Do you believe Jesus rose from the dead?

_____

_____

_____

Do you think the Bible is the Word of God?

_____

_____

_____

Yes and No Answers

Wherever possible, avoid questions that may be answered with a simple yes or no.

☐ Reword this question to avoid yes and no answers. Do you think that Judas thought Jesus would allow the officials to kill him?

_____

_____

_____

☐ Using the types of questions explained in the "Types of Questions" box, give an example here of each type of question. State what purpose or story you would use the question with.

Recall:
Story/purpose

_____

_____

Question

_____

_____

Organize data:
Story/purpose

_____

_____

Question

_____

_____

Analyze:
Story/purpose

_____

_____

Question

_____

_____

Judgment:
Story/purpose

_____

_____

Question

_____

_____

Speculate:
Story/purpose

_____

_____

Question

_____

_____

☐ Use the following form to help you evaluate the use of questions in a classroom situation. If you are currently teaching a class, tape a session and then listen to the tape, using the form for evaluation. If you are not currently teaching, visit a classroom for this evaluation.

Subject Title _____

Question _____

Answer(s)_____

Question _____

Answer(s)_____

Question _____

Answer(s)_____

Question _____

Answer(s)_____

Question _____

Answer(s)_____

Question _____

Answer(s)_____

Did the students seem to understand the questions? Comment:

_____

When a student asked a question, how did the teacher's response encourage thought?

_____

Was adequate thinking time allowed?

_____

Did the teacher jump right in to answer the question when no one responded immediately?

_____

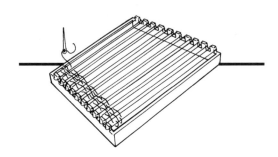

24 Teachable Moments

Purpose: To become alert to teachable moments in the class, no matter what the age-group.

If we understand that we teach persons and use curriculum as a tool, then it's easier to recognize and use the teachable moments. Sometimes these moments occur without our even realizing it, such as simply using the student's name or offering praise for some accomplishment. These acts teach the students that they are important and have abilities given to them by God, thus making them more receptive. Sometimes we call this the unwritten curricula.

In Conversations

There are many opportunities to teach spontaneously if you listen closely to what the student is saying and respond carefully. These exercises will help you think through such occasions.

☐ If the student tells you about something in nature he or she has observed, how can you incorporate God's plan into your answer?

_____

_____

☐ If the student speaks of going to the doctor or hospital, how can you answer and pass on the concept of medical personnel as God's helpers in healing?

_____

_____

_____

☐ If a student is worried about a test or some other trying situation, what can you say that includes prayer rather than "luck" or chance?

_____

_____

_____

In Relationships

God created us so that we are most fulfilled when in relationship with others and with God.

☐ If the student has been slighted or ridiculed, how can you help him or her recognize that God loves and understands, because Jesus went through the same thing?

_____

_____

_____

☐ How can you respond to a student's use of a racial slur in such a way as to help the student recognize that God is universal in character and loves us all equally?

_____

_____

_____

☐ When someone needs forgiveness, how can you encourage others to forgive that person, while expressing God's forgiveness?

_____

_____

_____

☐ What concept of God can you teach as you work with your class on some sort of guidelines or covenant between class members?

_____

_____

_____

News Items

We need to help students respond to all of life in a Christian way. That includes our response to the news that we hear and read about every day.

☐ Look in the newspaper or listen to the news and select several items that you can use as teachable moments. List the items here and record ways that you might turn them into learning experiences.

News Item	How It Might Be Made Teachable

At a Meal

A meal or snack can become routine. "Blessing" the food does not give it any special qualities, but it changes our attitude toward the food and toward God, who is ultimately responsible for our food.

☐ How can you use everyday words in a blessing in order to make God more personal to the students?

_____

_____

_____

☐ How can you help students express thanks to God for those persons responsible for growing and preparing our food?

_____

_____

_____

_____

☐ Look through your hymnal and locate suitable responses or songs used in worship. Use the lyrics with your class as blessings in order to increase their familiarity with the songs.

_____

_____

_____

Using Senses

Our senses are actually gifts from God. Being omnipotent, God could have made us without senses. God could have made the world in black and white and without any smell, sound, flavor, or texture.

☐ What experiences can you use to point out God's gift of smell?

_____

_____

_____

of sound?

_____

_____

_____

of sight?

_____

_____

_____

of taste?

_____

_____

_____

of touch?

_____

_____

_____

☐ How can you point out ways that God uses our senses as warnings?

_____

_____

_____

Seasons

Some geographic areas undergo drastic seasonal changes, and others subtle changes. The church seasons can also be used as teachable moments.

☐ How can you help students recognize the dependability of God using the change of seasons in nature?

_____

_____

_____

☐ How can you use the church seasons to strengthen a student's faith? (See page 82 for a study on the church seasons.)

Advent

_____

_____

Christmas

_____

_____

Epiphany

_____

_____

_____

Lent

_____

_____

_____

Easter

_____

_____

_____

Pentecost

_____

_____

_____

Other special days

_____

_____

_____

Worship Experiences

Worship is a time of encountering God. It might be called a time of awe or an "a-ha" experience with God, a time when we say, "Aha, I see God in that."

☐ List some times when you have unexpectedly encountered God.

_____

_____

_____

_____

☐ What sort of everyday experiences can lead to a statement or song of praise?

_____

_____

_____

☐ How can you bring everyday experience into the understanding of the sacraments? (A review of "The Sacraments" on page 75 might help.)

Baptism

_____

_____

_____

Communion

_____

_____

_____

Once you train your eye to be aware of the teachable moments, you will find them all around you, giving you rich opportunities to share Christ and help your students to grow in their faith.

Additional Resources

☐ For additional ideas and suggestions, review and read some of these books.

Halverson, Delia. *How Do Our Children Grow?* Nashville: Abingdon Press, 1993.
———. *Living Simply.* Nashville: Abingdon Press, 1996.
Halverson, Sam. *55 Group-Building Activities for Youth.* Nashville: Abingdon Press, 1996.

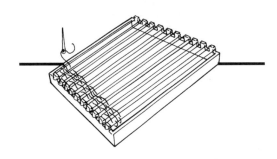

25 Teaching the Bible Creatively

Purpose: To learn ways to enhance the curriculum and weave the story into everyday experiences.

Often we think that simply drilling the words of the Bible into students' heads gives them Bible learning. Unless a person makes it a part of life, however, he or she may know every Bible verse by heart without true learning having taken place. The Bible gives us knowledge about what happened to the early witnesses of the faith, and it gives us inspiration. But it's more than a way to prove our beliefs; it is more than a defense of our faith. The Bible records how God has spoken to us through the years, and how God continues to speak.

☐ Read 2 Timothy 3:16-17. Pay special attention to the last half of this passage. What is the real reason that we teach the Bible?

_____

_____

_____

_____

_____

Adapting Curriculum

Creative teaching does not mean that you must start from scratch. By knowing your students you will discover which ones learn best in which ways.

☐ Read the section "Multiple Intelligence Learning" on page 42. What kinds of activities would be most appropriate for your students?

_____

_____

_____

_____

_____

It is important that the basic theme and scripture suggested in your curriculum be carried through in any changes you may make. Most published curriculum has a specific plan for introducing and reintroducing primary Bible passages. Skipping any of the passages will leave a gap in what is learned.

Three Guidelines

There are three guidelines suggested by Dorothy Jean Furnish in her book *Experiencing the Bible with Children* (Nashville: Abingdon Press, 1990, pp. 73-80). She suggests that each session include a "feeling into," a "meeting with," and a "responding out of" learning opportunity.

Select a lesson from your curriculum and look at the activities. Which ones fit into which category?

☐ *Feeling into*—to help students feel the same emotions as those felt by the characters in the story.

_____

_____

_____

☐ *Meeting with*—to help students feel as if they are on the spot.

_____

_____

_____

☐ *Responding out of*—to help students make use of their learnings in some way, expressing the story or planning some action that the story brings about.

_____

_____

_____

Everyday Experiences

☐ Become familiar with Bible stories so that you can share a story or verse spontaneously when the opportunity arises. Look up the following scripture passages and consider everyday experiences for which the passages might be used.

John 6:1-14

_____

_____

_____

Exodus 12

_____

_____

Luke 18:9-14

_____

_____

Mark 12:41-44

_____

_____

_____

Adapting Games

Curriculum for children and youth often provide games that help to teach the Bible. There are also many games you can purchase at Christian bookstores. However, it is simple to adapt nonbiblical games to Bible learning. Think of ways that these games might be changed to teach a particular (or several) scriptures.

☐ Concentration

_____

_____

_____

☐ Alphabet Game

_____

_____

_____

☐ Scavenger Hunt

_____

_____

_____

☐ Card Games

_____

_____

_____

_____

Drama

Teachers who have had little drama experience often ignore this method of teaching. The problem is that we too often feel that drama must be a polished play. In the classroom, learning comes about through the experience of living out situations (either biblical or from today). The learning is in the doing!

Jesus used drama when he broke bread with his disciples during the Passover meal. This drama helped the disciples connect his death with our salvation. Although they did not understand the drama at the time, what they had learned became evident to them later.

Drama can be as simple as acting out or responding to a question like, "How would you act in that situation?" or echoing words and movements. Older elementary children, youth, and adults will enjoy staging a reporter interview with known Bible characters or other persons—the "eyewitnesses" of an event.

Scripture passages can be modified into play readings. In play readings, parts are read instead of memorized, sometimes while the players simply sit on stools or walk through the actions. No production details are necessary, and older students require no practice time.

☐ Read Mark 4:35-41 and plan it as a play reading. Decide which verses should be read by which characters, and which by a narrator. You might even weave in opportunities for students to make sound effects.

_____

_____

_____

Art and Writing Activities

Both of these creative activities are used in Christian education to help students live out the scriptures. We use these activities because students learn through "doing." The finished product reinforces the learning at home, but the learning begins as they create. These activities also help the student get into a story and "move around" in the person's "shoes."

Older students respond to the use of research, which enhances learning. Some classes work with computers in their research.

Art and writing activities make for good "feeling into" and "responding out of" learning opportunities.

☐ Using crayons, paints, or colored markers, create two pictures:

Read Genesis 1:1-2 slowly. Then sit quietly with your eyes closed for two or three minutes, imagining what the earth would have been like when it was in chaos. Read Genesis 1:1-2 again, and express your feelings about the chaos in colors, not using structure or form.

Read Genesis 1:3-5. Again, sit quietly, but this time look at your first drawing and imagine the light breaking through the chaos. Again read Genesis 1:3-5 and draw or paint your expressions of God moving toward order by using the same colors as before and additional ones.

Various forms of writing help us to think through scripture. Paraphrase requires thinking through the specific passage in order to put it in our own words. Newspaper writing, letters, time lines, and poetry are other suggestions. Poetry does not need to rhyme. One of the easiest forms of poetry is the *cinquain* (sin-cane) poem.

☐ Read Luke 19:1-10 and select words or phrases that tell about the story, using the following form:

One-word title or subject   _____

Two words that tell about
the story   _____ _____

Three verbs or action words   _____ _____ _____

Four words telling of the
feeling about it   _____ _____ _____ _____

The subject word again, or another
word referring to the subject or title   _____

A word portrait expresses the feelings and experience of the person. A word portrait of the leper who returned to thank Jesus (Luke 17:11-19) might include descriptions of how the leper kept looking at his arms with disbelief.

☐ Select a Bible character and write a word portrait expressing feelings of the person on that occasion. Consider Luke 15:8-10 or John 21:7.

_____

_____

_____

_____

_____

_____

Music

Music has been a part of our heritage for as long as humans have tried to express themselves. Even if we are not strong in music, we can use it creatively in our teaching. If you don't feel comfortable leading singing, rely heavily on tape or CD players. Many instrumental recordings may be used as background or to help evoke feelings and emotions for the story.

☐ Take an inventory of your music collection or one that might be at the church, listening for music that you can use. As you listen, use the form that follows and begin a notebook or card file of the music.

Name of recording _____ Location _____

☐ Instrumental   ☐ Vocal   ☐ Nature sounds   ☐ Other sounds

How might it be used?

_____

_____

Subject?

_____

_____

Comments:

_____

_____

☐ One of the easiest ways to create songs is to use familiar melodies for stories from the Bible. Try some simple tunes such as "The Farmer in the Dell," "Doxology," and "Are You Sleeping, Brother John?"

☐ Learn this song to the tune of "Oats, Peas, Beans, and Barley Grow."

Pe-ter, John, and two named James,
An-drew, Mat-thew, Phi-lip too.
Tho-mas, Si-mon, Bar-thol-o-mew,
And Ju-das one and Ju-das two.[1]

Memorization

Many of us grew up with teachers who required that we memorize verses of scripture. Some of us struggled with each verse, and others found it an easy task. For those of us who have difficulty memorizing, often the problem is not a matter of application, but rather a difference in the way that we learn. Because of this, memorization should never be a matter of competition. Persons who have difficulty memorizing can become familiar with the passage when a class works at memorization together. However, be cautious about spending too much time on memorization if it shortens your time for experiencing the scripture.

Memorized verses can be pulled up for use conveniently. However, memorizing verses does not mean that they are learned. It is more important to understand the content than to be able to recite the words. We should learn the words in order to make use of the content in our daily life. Memorization is not a means in itself, but a means toward living our faith.

☐ Repetition helps memorization. What are some ways that you can incorporate repetition in your classroom?

_____

_____

_____

_____

☐ Create a litany about God's creation using the response "And God saw that it was good" (Gen. 1:12b).

_____

_____

_____

_____

☐ Songs and chants are good memorization tools. Review your hymnal and list several hymns that use portions of the Scriptures.

_____

_____

_____

☐ The Bible certainly isn't a children's book. In fact, most adults have considerable difficulty studying the Bible. If you teach children and youth, review *New Ways to Tell the Old, Old Story* by Delia Halverson (Abingdon Press). Pay special attention to the age level goals on page 15 and the suggested stories for specific ages on page 12.

Additional Resources

☐ Review some of these additional resources.

Benson, Dennis. *Creative Bible Studies,* 2 vols. Loveland, Colo.: Group Publishing, 1985, 1988.
Bruce, Barbara. *7 Ways of Teaching the Bible to Children.* Nashville: Abingdon Press, 1996.
Furnish, Dorothy Jean. *Adventures with the Bible.* Nashville: Abingdon Press, 1995.
———. *Experiencing the Bible with Children.* Nashville: Abingdon Press, 1990.
Griggs, Patricia. *Opening the Bible with Children.* Nashville: Abingdon Press, 1986.
Halverson, Delia. *How Do Our Children Grow?* Nashville: Abingdon Press, 1993.
———. *New Ways to Tell the Old, Old Story.* Nashville: Abingdon Press, 1992.
Smith, Judy Gattis. *26 Ways to Use Drama in Teaching the Bible.* Nashville: Abingdon Press, 1988.
Ward, Elaine M. *Growing with the Bible.* Prescott, Ariz.: Educational Ministries, 1986.
Wright, Chris. *User's Guide to the Bible,* rev. ed. Batavia, Ill.: Lion, 1994.

FINISHING THE FABRIC: PROJECTS FOR EACH STAGE OF STUDY

26 observe in the classroom

Usually, while we are teaching, we are not able to observe just how the students respond to us and to what is being taught. This is why it is important to observe a class being taught, whether you have taught in the past or not.

Arrange with a teacher to simply sit and observe.

Before the class, ask the teacher for the information in Part 1 of the form that follows. Part 2 will be used during class time. After the session, talk with the teacher, asking any questions you may have about the classroom experience.

Observation in a Classroom
Part 1

What scripture will be used? _____

What is the goal of the session?_____

What ages are the students? _____

Is there some special information about a particular student that will be helpful in understanding the class?

_____

Part 2

How was the goal for the session met?_____

Were the activities and materials appropriate for the age?_____

Comment:_____

_____

What variety of activities did you see?_____

_____

Was the room arrangement conducive to the activities and students?_____ how?_____

_____

_____

How were any discipline problems handled?_____

_____

What helped to make the worship time worshipful? What detracted from it?_____

_____

What "A-ha" moments did you witness, where a student came to a better understanding of the subject?

_____

What student seemed to lose interest? What was happening then?_____

_____

_____

Make additional comments._____

_____

From 32 WAYS TO BECOME A GREAT SUNDAY SCHOOL TEACHER
by Delia Halverson. Copyright © 1997 by Abingdon Press. Reproduced by permission.

27 Evaluate Your Class Session

We generally have a poor understanding of the evaluation process. It should be more positive than negative. A better term for the process is "debriefing." This is carried out best by looking at what went on, how the students interacted, and how the students grew in their faith. Review the following questions ahead of time so that you know what to look for during your session. Immediately after the session, fill out the form and use it as you plan your next session.

Date_____

Were the goals clear and attainable?_____

Did I reach them?_____

How, or why not?_____

_____

What went well about the session?_____

_____

Was there a particular problem or crisis during the session? How was it handled? How might you prevent such problems from happening again?_____

_____

What were some concerns that were expressed (verbally or nonverbally) by students during the session?_____

_____

How did you handle the concerns and how might you have handled them differently?_____

_____

How did particular students relate to other class members and to you as a teacher?_____

_____

Did all students participate? What was happening when students did not participate?_____

_____

How might you involve students who did not participate?_____

_____

Was the room set up adequately for the activities? How might it be set up better?_____

_____

Did you have all the materials you needed? What was missing?_____

_____

What did you learn about your students during this class?_____

_____

28 Act as Lead Teacher

The most effective learning comes as we teach or lead others. Your experience in the classroom will help less-experienced teachers or persons who are considering a teaching position. As you teach your class with other adults assisting you, you will learn even more about teaching, because you will be more conscious of your planning and what is happening in the classroom. If you do not have prospective teachers who can assist in this project, ask two or three of the parents of your students (or class members, if you teach adults) to assist. Use the following format as you plan, teach, and evaluate the class.

● Ask for their assistance to read the scripture, background materials, and lesson plans for the day, and to pray for God's guidance.

● Either meet with them or communicate by phone, asking their input about the lesson, such as any changes to the plan and what activities the students will or will not respond to.

● After you have adjusted the lesson plan (either together or with consultation), make sure that each person has a copy of the adjusted plan and knows just what responsibility he or she has.

● Assemble the materials needed and set up the room, with the help of your assistants if possible.

● Pray for your assistants, as well as your students.

● **Enjoy the teaching time!**

● After the session, debrief together and evaluate the session, using the form in Study 27, page 144.

● Thank those who worked with you, preferably in writing.

Session Date _____

Subject _____

Assistants who helped:

_____

_____

_____

_____

Observations about the session and about the leaders working together:

_____

_____

_____

_____

_____

_____

_____

_____

_____

29 Plan and carry out a Class Project

One of the best ways to create community in your class is to work together on a project that benefits others. This could be anything from the simple task of sorting cans at a food pantry or making greeting cards, to painting a classroom in your church or building a church in another country. You, as teacher, may lay the groundwork, but the class must have ownership in the project. It is best if the project grows out of your classroom learning experience. Follow this chart to think through the groundwork, and then use the next chart to keep track of the progress as you go along.

147

Groundwork for Class Project

Read a resource that can give you ideas for projects with the age level that you teach. Here are some suggestions. Books appropriate for children, youth, or adults are indicated by the letter in parentheses.

Beyond Leaf Raking by Peter Benson and Eugene Roehlkepartain, Abingdon Press. (Y)
Helping Children Care for God's People by Delia Halverson, Abingdon Press. (CY)
Leading Adult Learners by Delia Halverson, Abingdon Press. (A)
Mission and Event Annual, Cokesbury. (Y)
The Kid's Guide to Social Action by Barbara Lewis, Free Spirit Publishing. (CY)
The Kids Can Help Book by Suzanne Logan, Putnam Publishing. (C)

Read through your curriculum. Places in the study that may lend themselves to a project are:

_____   Study date: _____

_____   Study date: _____

_____   Study date: _____

_____   Study date: _____

_____   Study date: _____

Consider possible projects, and make contact with the proper persons for needed details.

Project-Address-Phone   **Information**

_____   _____

_____   _____

_____   _____

_____   _____

_____   _____

_____   _____

_____   _____

_____   _____

Class evaluation of proposed project: _____

_____

_____

Class Project

Goals for this event: _____

For participants: _____
For recipients: _____

Planning Committee Members	Phone
_____	_____
_____	_____
_____	_____
_____	_____

What sort of experience is the group capable of? (heavy or light physical work, VBS leadership, construction, medical or dental work, etc.): _____
_____

What ages will be involved in the actual work? (Will teenagers or children of families or parents of children be involved?):
_____

Will we need child care? _____ Whom will we get for this? _____
Length of time for event? _____
Date _____
Where (with what agencies) will this take place? _____
Transportation _____
Prior to event:
   Group-building activities: _____
_____

   Training activities:_____
_____

Dedication of mission (in worship, just before leaving, etc.): _____
_____

Church publicity plan:
_____
_____

Community publicity before and after (remember that publicity about your mission spreads Christ and your church's mission to the community): _____
_____

Event rules: _____
_____

Additional plans to be made (if coordinating your own work, consider supplies, equipment, schedules, lodging, food, spiritual enrichment, etc.): _____
_____

Budget: _____
Follow-up and evaluation: _____
_____

1

From 32 WAYS TO BECOME A GREAT SUNDAY SCHOOL TEACHER
by Delia Halverson. Copyright © 1997 by Abingdon Press. Reproduced by permission.

30 Compile Personal Teaching Files

Teachers who take their job seriously spend time accumulating materials that they can draw on as they prepare their lessons. These may be stories, games, songs, audiotapes, magazine articles, poetry, bibliographies on specific subjects, patterns, recipes, directions for activities, ideas for bulletin boards or banners, or anything else that might be of help in the future. You can find these helpful items in magazines, curriculum, newspapers, or handouts from workshops you will attend. Prepare file folders for these, using some of the following subjects and others that may be helpful to you. It helps to keep your subject and method file separate.

Subject file

- ☐ Baptism
- ☐ Bible
- ☐ Church history
- ☐ Communion
- ☐ Crisis and death
- ☐ Discipline
- ☐ Divorce
- ☐ Ethics
- ☐ Gambling
- ☐ Peer pressure
- ☐ Prayer
- ☐ Spirituality
- ☐ Talents-gifts

Method file

- ☐ Drama–role play
- ☐ Games
- ☐ Kite making
- ☐ Nature crafts
- ☐ Paper folding
- ☐ Paper mache
- ☐ Poetry writing
- ☐ Prints-printing
- ☐ Pottery
- ☐ Puppets
- ☐ Puzzles
- ☐ Recipes
- ☐ Stained glass

I will use the file subjects checked in the foregoing list, plus:

_____   _____

_____   _____

_____   _____

_____   _____

_____   _____

_____   _____

_____   _____

_____   _____

_____   _____

File completed:_____

31 Make a Permanent Teaching Aid

Teaching, like any other ministry, requires equipment. There are many economical ways to make items to aid you in your teaching, and you will reap the benefits later. Select one of the following or find instructions in other resources for a teaching aid that will be helpful to you. Laminate or preserve your teaching aid in some way, and store it carefully when not in use. This will save you time in the future when you want to use it again.

- **Flannel or felt board**—Cut heavy cardboard or plywood the desired size (about 30" × 24"). Cover it by gluing a large piece of flannel or felt to it, of a solid color (dark is best). Use colored fabric or plastic tape to finish the edges.

- **Pocket chart**—Use a large piece of poster board or heavy cardboard (22" × 28") and thirty-inch strips of three-inch-wide paper. Fold the long strips of paper in half, lengthwise, making them one and a half by thirty inches. At about five-inch intervals, place the paper strips across the poster board, with the folded edge at top. Fold the ends of the paper strips around the back of the poster board and secure with tape or glue. Tape the bottom edges of the paper strips securely to the front of the poster board. This forms shallow pockets for 3" × 5" cards. Write words or short phrases of a Bible verse on the tops of the cards so that the words show above the pockets. By placing these cards in the pockets in order, you have an aid to memorizing Bible verses. The class can read the verse together, then read it again and again, as a card is removed each time until you are saying it from memory.

- **Flat pictures**—Find pictures of nature, people in various activities, and so forth that can be used to spur conversation about specific subjects. Mount each picture on construction paper. These may be laminated for protection and then used many times. To use the pictures, spread them out on the floor or a table and ask the students to pick up one that reminds them of a specific subject you are studying. For example, you may ask them to pick up a picture that reminds them of the greatness of God, or of a person showing love. These are then shared with the group, or if you have a large class have them explain to a neighbor why they picked up the picture. Keep these for future use. The same pictures may be used for many different subjects.

- **Posters**—If there is a chart, poem, or some other item that you use from time to time (such as the books of the Bible), you will save time by making a nice poster with illustrations drawn or cut from magazines and laminating it for several uses.

- **Musical instruments**—Depending on student ages, some instruments can be made by the students themselves. Store them in a box for safekeeping from one class to another. (1) Rhythm sticks may be made from nine- to twelve-inch lengths of half-inch to one-inch dowels. Decorate them with colored markers or paints and protect with a coat of varnish. (2) Wrist or ankle bells may be used by attaching "jingle bells" to a one-inch elastic. (3) Drums can be made from oatmeal boxes, large economy-size cans, a wooden bucket or small keg, or use clay flowerpots of different sizes, or bottles or glasses filled with different amounts of water (for varying tones). Any of these may be tapped with wooden dowels. (4) Cymbals or shakers may be made with bells attached to aluminum pie tins, or small stones or beans placed between two paper plates stapled or taped together around the edges.

- **Symbol patterns**—Trace simple Christian symbols on poster board or lightweight cardboard. Cut them out and label them on the back. Laminate them for durability. These can be used for patterns in making banners or posters, or simply to recall and test student memories of the names and meanings of our symbols.

- **Puppets**—There are many books that give suggestions for making puppets. They can be made quite simply by removing the stuffing from the body and part of the head of a child's stuffed animal. By removing some of the stuffing from the front legs, you have places for fingers to work the legs. An old sock with a face drawn on using felt-tip markers also makes a good puppet.

- **Story hat**—Use any kind of hat and attach miniature items that remind us of a particular story (or of different parts of one story). These may be attached directly to the hat or hung from the hat with string. The hat is then used during the telling of the story.

- **Others**—Other projects might be biblical costumes, card or board games, echo pantomime stories, choral readings or litanies, songs, Bible bookmarks, time lines, a kiosk, mobiles, or posters.

☐ My teaching aid project is:

_____

_____

_____

☐ Completed on:

_____

32 Prepare and Teach Observation Sessions

In the early writings of scripture, we were given mandates for passing on the faith (Deut. 6:6-7; 31:12). As you finish this book, you are better prepared to carry out God's command. By teaching an observation class you will enable someone else to build skills to carry on the faith. Here are some guidelines to help you prepare for and teach such a class.

- You will want to prepare and teach the class in the same manner you would any other class, being certain that you attend to all details and prepare ahead.

- Follow the "Plan for Preparation" on page 107.

- Make a copy of the form titled "Observation in a Classroom" on page 142. Fill in part 1 and review part 2. Give this to the person or persons who will observe.

- Prepare the room and assemble supplies. Arrange for chairs for the observers to use. These need to be where they can observe most of what's happening in the room.

- If your class is made up of children or youth, explain to the students that the adults in the classroom are going to watch your class so that they can learn how to be better teachers.

- Enjoy teaching; don't worry about the observers. Your debriefing time with them will benefit from your natural, relaxed frame of mind.

- After the students have left, sit with the observers and discuss the notes that they took and any questions that might come up. Be honest, and if a question is asked that you can't answer, simply state that and make plans to seek the answer together. Make this a relaxed time, rejoicing in the learning process that has just taken place.

Observation class and date:

_____

Name of the observer or observers:

_____

_____

_____

_____

Your comments about the experience:

_____

_____

_____

_____

_____

APPENDIXES

PROGRESS CHART

Student Teacher-Weaver

☐ Why Christian Education?
☐ Ages and Stages
☐ (Optional Loom Study) _____
☐ (Choice of Warp Study) _____
☐ (Choice of Weft Study) _____
☐ (Choice of Weft Study) _____
☐ Project _____
☐ (Optional Project) _____

Congratulations! You may now study
for Apprentice Teacher-Weaver

Worker Teacher-Weaver

☐ Teaching Multiple Intelligences
☐ (Choice of Warp Study) _____
☐ (Choice of Weft Study) _____
☐ (Choice of Weft Study) _____
☐ Project _____
☐ (Optional Project) _____

Congratulations! You may now study
for Master Teacher-Weaver

Apprentice Teacher-Weaver

☐ How Faith Grows
☐ (Optional) How to Read and Study Bible Passages
☐ (Choice of Warp Study) _____
☐ (Choice of Weft Study) _____
☐ (Choice of Weft Study)
☐ Project _____

Congratulations! You may now study
for Worker Teacher-Weaver

Master Teacher-Weaver

☐ (Choice of Warp Study) _____
☐ (Choice of Warp Study) _____
☐ (Choice of Warp Study) _____
☐ (Choice of Weft Study) _____
☐ Project _____
☐ (Optional Project) _____

Congratulations! You are an accomplished
Master Teacher-Weaver

CERTIFICATE
OF
ACCOMPLISHMENT

This is to certify that, in response to God's calling to teach,

_____

has completed the following courses of study.

Student Teacher-Weaver   _____
                                                    Date

Apprentice Teacher-Weaver   _____
                                                    Date

Worker Teacher-Weaver   _____
                                                    Date

Master Teacher-Weaver   _____
                                                    Date

_____
(Church Name)

_____   _____
(Signed by Pastor)   (Signed by Education Representative)

Awarded this day _____

Notes

1. Ages and Stages

1. The adult segment of this survey is adapted from Delia Halverson, *Leading Adult Learners* (Nashville: Abingdon Press, 1995), pp. 24-26.

2. How Our Faith Develops

1. James W. Fowler, *Stages of Faith: The Psychology of Human Development and the Quest for Meaning* (New York: Harper & Row, 1981), chaps. 15–21.

2. Peter L. Benson and Carolyn H. Elkin, *Effective Christian Education: A National Study of Protestant Congregations* (Minneapolis: Search Institute, 1990).

3. How to Read and Study a Bible Passage

1. Dick Murray, *Teaching the Bible to Adults and Youth* (Nashville: Abingdon Press, 1993), p. 133, adapted and summarized.

5. Why Christian Education?

1. Peter L. Benson and Carolyn H. Elkin, *Effective Christian Education: A National Study of Protestant Congregations* (Minneapolis: Search Institute, 1990).

6. Enriching My Prayer Life

1. Delia Halverson, *Teaching Prayer in the Classroom* (Nashville: Abingdon Press, 1989), pp. 13-15.

2. Brother Lawrence, *The Practice of the Presence of God* (Springdale, Pa.: Whitaker House, 1982), pp. 8-9.

3. Delia Halverson, *Living Simply* (Nashville: Abingdon Press, 1996), pp. 111-12.

4. From Delia Halverson, "Teach Me How to Pray," *Youth!* magazine (February, 1990), Graded Press, p. 20.

8. Simplify, Simplify!

1. Delia Halverson, *Living Simply* (Nashville: Abingdon Press, 1996), pp. 55-56.

11. The Psalms

1. James Taylor, *Everyday Psalms* (Winfield, British Columbia: Wood Lake Books, 1994), p. 34.

12. The Sacraments

1. Delia Halverson, *Living Simply* (Nashville: Abingdon Press, 1996), p. 115.

2. Ibid., p. 116.

3. Ibid., pp. 112-13.

4. Ibid., p. 113.

13. Symbols of Christianity

1. Adapted from Delia Halverson, *How to Train Volunteer Teachers* (Nashville: Abingdon Press, 1991).

14. Worship

1. Delia Halverson, *How Do Our Children Grow?* (Nashville: Abingdon Press, 1993), pp. 112-13.

16. Incorporating Stewardship and Mission

1. Adapted from Delia Halverson, *Helping Children Care for God's People* (Nashville: Abingdon Press, 1994), pp. 17-19.

17. Learning Centers

1. Adapted from Delia Halverson, *How to Train Volunteer Teachers* (Nashville: Abingdon Press, 1991), Handout 17.

18. Lesson Planning

1. Delia Halverson, *How to Train Volunteer Teachers* (Nashville: Abingdon Press, 1991), p. 34.

19. Positive Classroom Atmosphere

1. Adapted from Delia Halverson, *How to Train Volunteer Teachers* (Nashville: Abingdon Press, 1991), Handout 8-B.

20. Prayer in the Classroom

1. Adapted from Delia Halverson, *Teaching Prayer in the Classroom* (Nashville: Abingdon Press, 1989), pp. 21-22.

2. Ibid., p. 53.

21. Selecting Curriculum for Adults

1. Adapted from Warren J. Hartman, *Five Audiences: Identifying Groups in Your Church* (Nashville: Abingdon Press, 1987), pp. 25-28.

23. Using Questions in Teaching

1. Delia Halverson, *Leading Adult Learners* (Nashville: Abingdon Press, 1995), p. 41.

25. Teaching the Bible Creatively

1. Delia Halverson, *New Ways to Tell the Old, Old Story* (Nashville: Abingdon Press), p. 62.

29. Plan and Carry Out a Class Project

1. Delia Halverson, *Leading Adult Learners* (Nashville: Abingdon Press, 1995), pp. 86-87.